Pandaemonium

For Charles Blitzer

Also by Daniel Patrick Moynihan

On the Law of Nations

Came the Revolution: Argument in the Reagan Era

Family and Nation

Loyalties

*Counting Our Blessings: Reflections
on the Future of America*

A Dangerous Place

Ethnicity: Theory and Experience
(Editor, with Nathan Glazer)

Coping: Essays on the Practice of Government

The Politics of a Guaranteed Income

On Equality of Educational Opportunity
(Editor, with Frederick Mosteller)

*On Understanding Poverty: Perspectives
from the Social Sciences* (Editor)

Toward a National Urban Policy (Editor)

*Maximum Feasible Misunderstanding:
Community Action in the War on Poverty*

*The Defenses of Freedom: The Public Papers
of Arthur J. Goldberg* (Editor)

*Beyond the Melting Pot: The Negroes,
Puerto Ricans, Jews, Italians, and Irish
of New York City* (with Nathan Glazer)

DANIEL PATRICK
MOYNIHAN

Pandaemonium

Ethnicity in
International
Politics

OXFORD UNIVERSITY PRESS

Oxford University Press, Walton Street, Oxford OX2 6DP

Oxford New York
Athens Auckland Bankok Bombay
Calcutta Cape Town Dar es Salaam Delhi
Florence Hong Kong Istanbul Karachi
Kuala Lumpur Madras Madrid Melbourne
Mexico City Nairobi Paris Singapore
Taipei Tokyo Toronto
and associated companies in
Berlin Ibadan

Oxford is a trade mark of Oxford University Press

Published in the United States by
Oxford University Press Inc., New York

First published in hardback 1993
Reprinted 1993 (twice)
First published in paperback 1994
Reprinted 1994

British Library Cataloguing in Publication Data
Data available

Library of Congress Cataloging in Publication Data
Moynihan. Daniel P. (Daniel Patrick). 1927–
Pandaemonium: ethnicity in international politics / Daniel
Patrick Moynihan.
p. cm.
Includes bibliographical references.
1. World Politics—1989-. 2. Ethnicity. 3. Nationalism.
4. Ethnic relations. I. Title.
D860.M69 1993 909.82—dc20 92–41370
ISBN 0–19–827787–3
ISBN 0–19–827946–9 (pbk)

Printed on acid-free paper in
The United States of America

PREFACE

*P*ANDAEMONIUM was written as a warning. It appeared to me that the world was entering a period of ethnic conflict, following the relative stability of the cold war. This could be explained. As large formal structures broke up, and ideology lost its hold, people would revert to more primal identities. Conflict would arise based on these identities. Indeed, the world had already been introduced to the term "ethnic cleansing." In a wondrously generous letter, the eminent scientist Edward O. Wilson wrote to say that "a coiled and ready ethnicity is to be expected from a consideration of biological evolutionary theory." Once "the overwhelmingly suppressive force of supranational ideology was lifted" ethnicity would strike. "It was an unintended experiment in the natural science mode: cancel one factor at a time, see what happens." See the rape of Bosnia.

At about this time, James Q. Wilson published his magisterial reflection, *The Moral Sense.* Is there, he asks, anything that can be judged a universal moral sense? He answers that there is and that it resides in the universal need for a sense of solidarity with others. This need originates with family and of its own ascends only so far.

What makes Serbs, Croats, Slovaks, Ghegs, Tosks, Armenians, Kurds, Bantus, Masai, Kikuyus, Ibos, Germans, and countless—literally countless—other peoples argue, fight, and die for "ethnic self-determination"? Why do they seek to be ruled by "one's own kind" when what constitutes "one's own kind" is so uncertain and changeable, being variously defined as people whom you think are like you in language, customs, place or origin, and perhaps other, inexpressible, things as well? . . . For some reason, the need for affiliation is so powerful that it reaches as far as one can find a historically plausible and emotionally satisfying principle of similarity.

In a personal communication he continues:

[E]recting walls that separate "us" from "them" is a necessary correlate of morality since it defines the scope within which sympathy, fairness, and duty operate. The chief wall is the family/clan/village, but during certain historical periods ethnicity (an *abstract* family, clan, or village) defines the wall.

The great achievement of Western culture since the Enlightenment is to make many of us peer over the wall and grant some respect to people outside it; the great failure of Western culture is to deny that walls are inevitable or important.

A radical thought; as Wilson insists. And yet after a century of marginalization and, now, in American universities, trivialization, it is *time* for radical thought. In late 1992, whilst *Pandaemonium* was in press, I made my way into Sarajevo and thereafter to parts of Bosnia and Croatia. I had had some acquaintance with the region and so was struck by the ethnic obsession of the peoples there. All things past, present, future were to be explained in these terms only. I visited the coastal town of Slano on the Adriatic. It has been occupied by Montenegrins. There was nothing left save the handwriting on the ruined walls. In roman letters, so that Croatians would be sure to understand (Montenegrins speak the same language but use the Cyrillic alphabet), the graffiti declared that what had happened was reasoned vengeance for past wrong. One warrior named Marko, concerned that his message go beyond the borders of Croatia, had scrawled in English "YOU ASK FOR IT." The slight error in tense seemed to say it all. Your very existence makes me hate you.

Gentle reader, go warily into this perilous land.

DANIEL PATRICK MOYNIHAN

Pindars Corners, New York
September 4, 1993

ACKNOWLEDGMENTS

*I*T was the greatest honor to be invited by Oxford University to give the 1991 Cyril Foster Lecture, and the greatest pleasure to be welcomed there by Professor Adam Roberts, who served first as my host and then as my advisor as the lecture turned into a book. All that could be done to save me from error, he did. I alone am responsible for the no doubt considerable number that remain. Stephen Rickard was as much collaborator as arbiter of legal questions, national and international. I hope he knows my indebtedness to him. Joshua Levine and Paula Jacobson were relentless research assistants. As for Eleanor Suntum, there are no adequate words.

D.P.M.

FOREWORD

*T*HIS book is a witty and wise survey of a tragic set of subjects: the all-too-central role of ethnicity and nationalism in international politics; the ways in which doctrines of national self-determination—fine in theory—can provide a recipe for almost limitless conflict; and the dismal failure of so many people, who should have known better, to understand the strength and significance of ethnicity.

Senator Moynihan gave the 1991 Cyril Foster lecture at Oxford on 29 November 1991. The lecture was no pedantic plod: pedestrianism would hardly be appropriate when the subject is Pandaemonium, nor likely when the lecturer is Daniel Patrick Moynihan. At times breathtakingly discursive, always idiosyncratic, it was a series of brilliant flashes which illuminated a funny, sad, and muddled aspect of our intellectual and political landscape. It ranged freely over time as well as space. It was even, dare one say it, profound. Though much expanded from its earlier incarnation, this book has retained these notable qualities.

The sombre background to both lecture and book is the collapse, which became complete in late 1991 and early 1992, of both the Soviet Union and of the Socialist Federal Republic of Yugoslavia. The aftermath of empires is almost always violent. When familiar if unloved structures crumble, new states emerge—often lacking legitimate political systems and legitimate frontiers. At least up to 1989–90 the decline of communism as a ruling ideology was remarkably peaceful, but many of the post-Communist events in these countries have been violent. The power of ethnic politics, the revival of ancient ethnic antagonisms, the impossibility of satisfying competing claims for self-determination—these are a major part of the reason for the fighting, the sieges, and the terrible cruelties that have ensued.

The disorder in the ex-U.S.S.R. and ex-Yugoslavia has in one major respect been even greater than that following the great European decolonizations of the post-1945 period: this time, many of the successor entities showed almost immediate signs of fission. The boundaries inherited from European colonialism in Asia and Africa, widely criticized as artificial imperial impositions, survived decolonization a great deal better than some of the once-internal boundaries of the Soviet Union and Yugoslavia; where ethnic politics, partially concealed in the Communist era, were returning with redoubled vengeance.

The evils that ensued in these ex-countries more than justify Moynihan's title. In Milton's *Paradise Lost*, Pandaemonium was the high capital of Satan and his peers:

High on a throne of royal state . . .

> Satan exalted sat, by merit raised
> To that bad eminence . . .

Or, as Moynihan puts it towards the end of his text, Pandaemonium was inhabited by demons who were quite convinced that the Devil had their best interests in mind. If the force of nationalism, and the idea of national self-determination, are high on a throne today, at least in some parts of the world, it is by merit: they are responses to real problems, and to the experience of imperial arrangements. Yet their eminence is indeed bad. The title perfectly captures the ambivalent nature of the subject-matter.

This is a study, not of the origins of ethnicity, but of its place in our intellectual and political life. None the less, the reader may ask: What exactly is the ethnicity which is the subject of this book? How does it relate to the overlapping but distinct phenomenon of nationalism? Moynihan gives many clues, but does not rush into definitions. He will no doubt be criticized for this. However, it is the essence of international politics that there are quite different interpretations of forces and events. Definitions may clarify an author's intent, but are unlikely to command universal assent. The term "ethnicity" easily suggests that criteria pertaining to race and language are decisive in determining group identity. However, some deep conflicts of our time involve rival groups which are of similar or identical race and language—as in Northern Ireland, or (if to a lesser extent) in some of the terrible conflicts in Yugoslavia. In these cases, what binds a group together, separates it from others, and fatefully leads it into action, is not just (and perhaps not at all) language, or religion, or skin-color, but also a sense of common vulnerability: past history and present experience teach who are one's enemies, and who one's friends. Security is thus one major key to identity. Whether or not it is right to apply the term "ethnic" to all these conflicts is not very important.

The significance of Moynihan's book lies first of all in its emphatic assertion of the continuing and tragic importance of ethnic issues—however defined—not only in international relations, but also in the domestic politics of states. There have not been many wars in this century whose origins do not include interethnic hostility in some form, and the failure of national boundaries to reflect ancient or modern ethnic realities.

In the post-1945 period, many people—mesmerized by Cold War—took the view that the conflict between democracies and communism was the main issue of world politics. This view was especially prevalent in the U.S.A. Moynihan always had his doubts, as was evident in many of his public pronouncements and in the book he co-edited in 1975, *Ethnicity: Theory and Experience*. As he reminds us in the present text, he foresaw the breakup of the Soviet empire a decade before it happened. When in early 1992 he presented a doubting Henry Kissinger with evidence that some people at least had seen what was coming in the Soviet Union, he received what is probably the shortest, and certainly the humblest, letter from his former Harvard and government colleague:

April 2, 1992

Dear Pat:

I stand corrected. Your crystal ball was better than mine.

Warm regards,
Henry A. Kissinger

Coming from his intellectual background (just like Kissinger from *his*), Moynihan was not inclined to join those who thought that the end of the Cold War was in any sense the end of history. In this he was sadly right. There has been all too much history in the short time since the Cold War finally expired at some point in the years 1989–91.

Moynihan's text also points to some special factors which make Americans ill-prepared to come to terms with the central role that ethnicity plays in international politics. Being based, however imperfectly, on individual rather than group rights and on the idea of the melting pot, the U.S.A. is often inclined to underestimate the elemental force of ethnic issues elsewhere. The idea that there is nothing wrong with the peoples of the world, only with their governments, is deeply attractive; but perhaps the day should dawn when an American President gets his lines wrong and says: "We have no quarrel with the government of X, only with the people." Or perhaps "peoples."

There is confusion in the very language that not only Americans, but also others, use in describing the world. By a routine and understandable fiction, the word "nation" is regularly employed to refer to any foreign state, whether or not the peoples who inhabit it are a cohesive group with some sense of shared identity. Even the Soviet Union and Yugoslavia were sometimes called "nations." Not just in these egregious cases, but also in others, the word "country" might usefully be dragged back into service as a more honest substitute. The way in which we use words—especially perhaps the word "nation"—is important. We cannot change the name of the United Nations, nor the many odd uses of the word "international," but we can be more conscious of the awkward fact that states and nations are by no means always co-terminous.

What are the policy implications of Moynihan's analysis? They are many, even if they are simple; and his analysis deserves attention from European policymakers, many of whom have not exactly covered themselves with glory in the numerous ethnic conflicts of our continent and its off-shore islands.

Moynihan is particularly interesting on the implications for U.S. foreign policy. If international politics consists largely, not of a Manichean struggle of right versus wrong, but of impossibly competing ethnic identities and mutually incompatible dreams of national self-determination, might this not reinforce American disenchantment, not just with the supposed New World Order, but with all involvement in a hopelessly benighted world? A U.S. Senator can and will answer for himself, but any such isolationist conclusion is a good deal simpler than Moynihan's rich text warrants. He reminds us, if briefly, that the world has seen many successes in interethnic relations, which have taken many forms; and that affluence has often proved a surprisingly good modern cure for ancient ethnic animosity. The very fact that the most virulent forms of nationalism are often unleashed by the collapse of external frameworks (one dare not use the word "empire" with reference to America) must reinforce the doubt about rushing into isolation. Rather, this survey is a plea for a better understanding of nationalism, for knowing when to ride with it as well as against it, and for a more informed international discussion of that fateful slogan-doctrine, to which the United States and the Soviet Union both in their ways subscribed, of national self-determination.

If, beyond that, no simple and universally applicable policy recommendations emerge from this study, Senator Moynihan is in good company. When in 1961 the late Elie Kedourie published the second edition of his book on *Nationalism*, he wrote a preface containing these words:

Noticing the first edition, some reviewers have remarked that I do not attempt to discuss whether nationalists should be conciliated or resisted. A decision on such an issue is necessarily governed by the particular circumstances of each individual case, and whether its consequences are fortunate or disastrous will depend on the courage, shrewdness and luck of those who have the power to take it.

Moynihan would, I suspect, sympathize with this caution; but his excursion into this field none the less comes at a good time, and will be of value in many debates about policy—and not just in the U.S.A. In his last chapter, he suggests that the U.N. needs to set about fashioning approaches to conflicts concerning self-determination. In a way, the U.N. has begun to do so. In *An Agenda for Peace*, the essay on the U.N.'s future role which Secretary-General Boutros-Ghali issued on 17 June 1992, it is stated in paragraphs 17 to 19:

The United Nations has not closed its door. Yet if every ethnic, religious or linguistic group claimed statehood, there would be no limit to fragmentation, and peace, security and economic well-being for all would become ever more difficult to achieve.

One requirement for solutions to these problems lies in commitment to human rights with a special sensitivity to those of minorities, whether ethnic, religious, social or linguistic . . . The General Assembly soon will have before it a declaration on the rights of minorities. That instrument, together with the increasingly effective machinery of the United Nations dealing with human rights, should enhance the situation of minorities as well as the stability of States.

. . . The sovereignty, territorial integrity and independence of States within the established international system, and the principle of self-determination for peoples, both of great value and importance, must not be permitted to work against each other in the period ahead.

These formulae raise as many problems as they solve; and they might get a wry smile from Senator Moynihan, whose period as U.S. Ambassador to the U.N. (1975–6) no doubt reinforced his appreciation of that great feature of modern international law and organization: the simultaneous propounding of two equal and opposite principles. Yet the Secretary-General's words do clearly identify a central problem of the post-Cold-War world. They also point to the urgent need for a richer and more nuanced international debate about ethnicity, nationalism, and self-determination: a cause which is notably advanced by Moynihan's engaging study.

ADAM ROBERTS

Balliol College, Oxford
August 1992

CONTENTS

INTRODUCTION

*T*HE will of Cyril Foster asks that Oxford University arrange for a "sincere speaker to deliver once every year a lecture . . . dealing with the elimination of war and the better understanding of the nations of the world." On being invited to give the 1991 lecture, I sought to take advantage of a certain ambiguity in that devise. "[T]he better understanding of the nations of the world." Ought that refer to better understanding *between* the nations of the world? Or to a better understanding *of* them? Obviously either. I chose the latter as my subject and was forthwith engaged with a further ambiguity. What exactly is a nation?

There is no correct answer to this question; none that you could look up. But therein lies the importance of the question and its relation to the "elimination of war." The subject is one of profound and all too frequently murderous dispute. Walker Connor, following Max Weber, defines a nation as "a group of people who *believe* they are ancestrally related. It is the largest grouping that shares that belief."[1] The key question as Connor defines it is not what is a nation, but when.

The delay—in some cases stretching into centuries—between the appearance of national consciousness among sectors of the elite and its extension to the masses reminds us of the obvious but all-too-often ignored fact that nation-formation is a process, not an occurrence or event. . . . Events are easily dated; stages in a process are not. . . . There is no formula. . . . [T]he point at which a quantitative addition in the number sharing a sense of common nationhood has triggered the qualitative transformation into a nation resists arithmetic definition.[2]

A further stage is reached when we come to the nation state; a nation matched with territory. This is what nineteenth-century European nationalism was about, notably the unification of first Italy, then Germany. Something similar happened in France. Eugen Weber has traced that process with wondrous clarity in his *Peasants into Frenchmen: The Modernization of Rural France, 1870–1914.* (French was considered a foreign language by roughly half the population that came of age in France in the last quarter of the nineteenth century.)[3] It is a commonplace of American immigration studies that most of the "new" immigrants who began to arrive from Eastern and Southern Europe in 1880 or thereabouts learned of their previous nationality only after settling in the United States. Again Connor:

There is ample evidence that Europe's currently recognized nations emerged only very recently, in many cases centuries later than the dates customarily assigned for their emergence. In the matter of nation-formation, there has been far less difference in the timetables of Western and Eastern Europe than is customarily acknowledged, and the lag time between

Europe and the Third World has also been greatly exaggerated.
Indeed, in the case of a number of putative nations within
Europe, it is problematic whether nationhood has even yet
been achieved.[4]

Thus, while Russia has recognized Moldova to be a
distinct nation, will Rumania continue to? And whilst the
world was elsewhere engaged, the success of the Marxist
rulers in Tirana in forging an Albanian nationality out
of highland Gegs and southerly Tosks remains
problematic.

The Gegs and Tosks of the world represent a further
complexity which is worldwide, or virtually so.
Nationalism arose in nineteenth-century Europe as an
exercise in matching a "people" with a state. This was
new to Europe and virtually unknown in most of the rest
of the world where sovereignty rested on quite different
principles of legitimacy. Gegs and Tosks, descendants of
the Illyrians, enter the twentieth century as subjects of
the Ottoman Empire. As of 1967, when Albania declared
itself to be the world's only officially atheist state, 27
percent of the population was Christian, with rather
more Eastern Orthodox than Roman Catholic. The rest
was Muslim, divided about equally between Sunni Gegs
and Sunni or Bektashi Tosks. Geg and Tosk are the two
divisions of the Albanian branch of the Indo-European
family of languages. They are close to the Hellenic and
the Italic families, but distant from Balto-Slavic. Their
respective regions are roughly divided by the Shkumbin
River, which flows from the mountains to the Adriatic
about midpoint in the country. Gegs, however, spill over
into the province of Kosovo in the former Yugoslavia and

as far north and east as Serbia. Albanian independence was proclaimed in 1912, making it one of the older states in the twentieth-century roster, but thoroughly representative. Virtually the whole of Africa and much of Asia and Europe is made up of states that were once part of vast empires, now broken up. Most are multi-lingual, most have distinctive regions, most have internal strife. As do most of the states of the Western Hemisphere, albeit within a distinctive pattern. Are these states "nations" as we have just defined the term?

Clearly not. But they *are* states. Members of an organization of states which, to obscure matters, is called the United Nations. Here we enter the realm of political myth, useful or otherwise. The Charter begins: "WE THE PEOPLES OF THE UNITED NATIONS." The reference is clearly to the American Constitution and the still-revolutionary idea that a people is defined by belief rather than blood, and for that matter, political belief. The Charter goes on to imply a distinction between people and government. The Preamble to the Charter, having set forth the aims of the organization, reverts to capital letters—"HAVING RESOLVED TO COMBINE OUR EFFORTS TO ACCOMPLISH THESE AIMS"—and the document is accordingly agreed to by representatives of "our respective Governments."

There is no surmounting these ambiguities; they reflect reality. To tidy up the taxonomy would merely distort reality. However, as our title indicates, I believe it is helpful to distinguish between ethnic group and nation, between ethnicity and nationality. It is a distinction of degree. The nation is the "highest" form of the ethnic group, denoting a subjective state of mind as regards ancestry, but also, almost always, an objective

claim to forms of territorial autonomy ranging from a
regional assembly to full-blown independence. Nation
states no longer seem inclined to go to war with one
another, but ethnic groups fight all the time. Inevitably,
many of these ethnic clashes make their way into the
realm of international politics.

I accept that this usage could reflect an overly
American perspective. The author participated in some of
the early discussions that led to publication of the
magisterial *Harvard Encyclopedia of American Ethnic
Groups*, edited by Stephan Thernstrom and Ann Orlov.
And yet, the usage is not simply American. On May 14,
1992, Mikhail Gorbachev spoke to members of the
United States Congress in Statuary Hall of the Capitol.
He spoke of the violence erupting in so many parts of the
former Soviet Union, making a nice distinction between
ethnicity and nationality.

One problem which is assuming an acute and at times
dramatic character in Russia is that of ethnic enclaves which,
thanks to the breakup of the formerly unified state organism,
are being violently separated from their accustomed mother-
land, and now find themselves on the other side of a national
boundary. This is true first and foremost of Russians, but also
of other nationalities which are organically connected with
Russian culture, the Russian language and the Russian way of
life.

The situation is aggravated by the paroxysms of extreme
nationalism which have here and there generated direct
discrimination against minorities. Sometimes this is carried to a
point which resembles apartheid. In this situation, any
incautious step by anyone, however well intended it might be,
can be misinterpreted and used in a way contrary to what was

anticipated. And of course, any actions which contradict extraterritorial principles of human rights, should be called by their true name. Assistance here by the United States, United Nations or the European Community would be no less significant than the West's humanitarian food assistance. We must also recognize that no Russian government can ignore discrimination against a Russian-speaking population, especially when this leads to armed clashes and to the creation of hundreds of thousands of refugees. If the democrats cannot resolve this problem it will be resolved by totalitarian nationalists. It can hardly be in the interest of the United States not to consider this circumstance in its relations with Russia and the other states of the commonwealth.[5]

He went on to speak of the "broader issue of European instability," an instability deriving from the ethnic conflict that was succeeding "the long peace," in John Lewis Gaddis's phrase, of the cold war.

Having thus chosen my topic, and sorted out, as much as I shall ever do, some matters of usage, I set to work on this essay in the summer of 1991. Simultaneously, I entered upon a thought experiment, if that is a permissible term. Recall that Oxford would require a "sincere speaker" who would address himself to "the better understanding of the nations of the world." I resolved that as the work progressed I would continuously consult *The Economist*, which is frequently sincere and invariably a source of better understanding. *The Economist* would be my guide to the conduct of ethnic groups, nations, nation states in what clearly was to be a new world.

Forty years ago when I began reading *The Economist* as a graduate student at the London School of Economics and Political Science, its pages were filled with accounts of ideological conflict, most of it reflecting the seeming inexorable onset of an armageddonic clash between the Leninist states of the Eurasian heartland and the more or less democratic states on the periphery. *The Economist*, of course, was a conservative paper, much as the political science faculty at L.S.E. was in the main conservative. Both detesting communism, whilst at the same time over-estimating the strength of communist regimes. Neither the newspaper nor the scholars were "threat enhancers" of the sort that would generally hold sway in Washington in the decades ahead. But both *were* economics-minded, and were not wholly dismissive of Marxist-Leninist claims concerning the greater efficiency of socialist production. But by the 1920s we had said goodbye to all that. I thereupon hypothesized that the then current *Economist* would be filled with accounts of *ethnic* conflict.

I do not mean to suggest that there was anything rigorous in this "thought experiment." I was merely curious to see how much would be revealed by a random sampling of the week's news. I was writing then, as I am now, in a schoolhouse in upstate New York. I accordingly sent to Washington for the then current *Economist* (August 10, 1991) and to no very great surprise found my forecast confirmed. The cover story was entitled, "Here Lies Yugoslavia." It depicted the onset of tribal violence in that region. The lead editorial began: "Two ideas are dying in the Balkan bloodshed. One is the belief that Yugoslavia . . . can be put together again as it was. The other is the hope that, in the new Europe, common sense and common interests would make war unthinkable."[6] Indeed, by autumn, war seemed the only thing

"Yugoslavs" *could* think about. (At the end of November, an editorial in the *New York Times* would begin: "To Guernica, Coventry, Stalingrad and Dresden the world may now add Vukovar and Dubrovnik.")[7]

The next *Economist* leader in that issue, "Whose Jerusalem," shed but little light on this difficult question, but made it sufficiently clear that the question was not about to go away. Further into the week's issue we learned that a number of Hindu Asians expelled from Uganda in 1972 by ex-President Idi Amin were now returning. East Africa had generally applauded the expulsion. This because "In Uganda, Tanzania and Kenya, people from the Indian subcontinent had long played the unpopular role that Jews once played in Eastern Europe." But "the mass nationalisation programmes of the 1970s" hadn't worked.[8] (Which put me in mind of a visit to Mandalay in 1973 while I was serving as U.S. Ambassador to India. Driving about the city in our one consular car, I came upon a small enclave in which all the signs were in Chinese. I remarked on this to my Burmese guide, who explained: "Before independence everything in Burma was owned by Chinese and Indians. That is why we had to have socialism.") Meanwhile, back in the Balkans, another *Economist* story told of various European efforts to intervene in Yugoslavia in a peacekeeping mode. But a British minister had sniffed that "You can't have peacekeepers if there's no peace to keep." There was a "vague threat" of military force from Russia. But not to worry: "The optimists point out that this is not 1914 . . . . "[9]

Well, yes. But then consider that in 1914 the optimists contended it was not 1914. Would it not be at least as useful to consider the possibility that the world is in a significant sense back at that juncture in history and that this time we might make a better job of it?

Obviously, we are at an end of the seventy-five year crisis of the European state system that went on from 1914 to 1989. Just as obviously, there is a halo effect as political and economic liberalism makes its way from capital to capital around the world in the manner of 1848. The age of totalitarianism is ended. That claim to the future, is over. The obvious question then is what ought we expect now? We should surely resume the business of trying to advance a rational, liberal, legal world order that was so much on display even to the moment the lights went out in Europe in 1914. This was the central argument of another long essay, *On the Law of Nations*, which I wrote in the summer of 1989 when that structure of totalitarian expectation was crashing the world over.[10] The Marxist-Leninist ideas that *The Economist* once described as threatening to take the twentieth century by storm, of a sudden seemed hardly to have existed. With the fog of the cold war lifting, I argued that the United States, and others of course, would now once again recognize the enormous importance and our own great interest in a new world order based on old legal principles. This was a reasonable enough argument, and timely enough. (In the summer of 1990 with the invasion of Kuwait, the President of the United States took to invoking "international law," the "rule of law," and Chapter VII of the United Nations Charter, as if such terms were part of the working vocabulary of American statecraft.[11] In fact, they had all but disappeared.) But the argument was incomplete. It did not deal with a yet larger question: Why *did* the lights go out at Sarajevo?

F. H. Hinsley begins his fine study, *Nationalism and the International System*, by noting the irony that among a range of formidable scholars, those who made a particular study of nationalism tended to ascribe the outbreak of World War I to "war parties" in imperial capitals, whilst those who made a particular study of the international system tended to ascribe the outbreak to nationalism.[12] Thus, in the 1930s, Elie Halévy contended that from the turn of the century some forces encouraged revolution and others enhanced the prospects for war. These latter were the forces of nationalism, "the principle of nationality."[13] Anticipating Seymour Martin Lipset, Halévy argued that as the great powers grew more industrialized, they would seek peace among themselves. But this influence had been defeated by "other forces, non-economic in their nature and stronger than industrialism."[14] A generation later Bernadotte Schmitt, in *The Origins of the First World War* (1958), would agree: "The primary cause of the war was a conflict between political frontiers and the distribution of peoples, the denial of. . . the right of [national] self-determination. . . . More than any other circumstances, this conflict between existing governments and their unhappy minorities was responsible for the catastrophe of 1914."[15] Whatever the case, war came and the world changed—utterly.

There are today just eight states on earth which both existed in 1914 and have not had their form of government changed by violence since then. These are the United Kingdom, four present or former members of the Commonwealth, the United States, Sweden, and Switzerland.[16] Of the remaining 170 or so contemporary states, some are too recently created to have known much recent turmoil, but for the greater number that have done, far the most frequent factor involved has been ethnic conflict.

Yet, it is possible to have studied international relations through the whole of the twentieth century and hardly to have noticed this. The word ethnicity appears in the 1933 edition of the *Oxford English Dictionary* as *Obs. rare*. It is defined as "Heathendom, heathen superstition"—that is, something of the past, long vanished. It does not appear in the first edition of *The Fontana Dictionary of Modern Thought*.[17] Clearly, we have a subject here that had to struggle to make its way into the modern sensibility. Donald L. Horowitz has summed up: "Connections among Biafra, Bangladesh, and Burundi, Beirut, Brussels, and Belfast were at first hesitantly made—isn't one 'tribal,' one 'linguistic,' another 'religious'?—but that is true no longer. Ethnicity has fought and bled and burned its way into public and scholarly consciousness."[18] There is no escaping the ultimate question of statehood, not, that is, in the present age, but the prior condition of mere ethnic attachment is a legitimate subject of its own. Hinsley takes us far back, and properly so.

As an ethnic or cultural group the nation, like the family, the clan, the tribe and other ethnic and cultural groups, is primordial: the earliest extant texts in Hittite, Vedic Sanskrit and Mycenaean Greek all contain a word for it. And the Romans were following all earlier usage when they pronounced the Jews to be a *natio*, as also the Greeks and the assemblage of German tribes, because it was not as Jews, Greeks or Germans that they were politically organised. In the same way, they did not regard themselves, the Romans, as a *natio*, precisely because they were politically organised as tribes, as a city-state or as an empire, on lines that made the word irrelevant to them.[19]

Clearly, there are no more Romes. Nor Holy Roman Empires. Nor, as Charles Blitzer observes, did the rambling, multi-ethnic Westphalian state mark the end of history, which would seem to be moving to yet larger combinations such as the European Community and simultaneously to much smaller ethnic entities. There is surely something to be learned from the experience of the former Soviet Union. In 1992 Boris N. Yeltsin, as President of the newly established Russian Federation, told a Joint Meeting of the United States Congress, "Russia is a founding member of the Commonwealth of Independent States which has averted uncontrolled disintegration of the former empire and the threat of a general inter-ethnic bloodbath."[20] If bad enough, the experience clearly could have been worse. As was clearly very much in the minds of those involved.

If scholars tended to overlook or ignore these matters, bartenders had a way of spotting them even so. Thus, towards the close of the last century, there was much talk in the United States about the "Anglo-Saxon race" and its manifest, multitudinous virtues. From his vantage point behind the bar of his saloon on Ar-rchey Road in Chicago, Mr. Dooley observed to "Hinnissy" that "An Anglo-Saxon . . . is a German that's forgot who was his parents."[21] (In the 1990 Census more Americans reported German ancestry, 19.6 percent, than any other.

Irish at 13.1 percent was the runner-up with English, 11 percent, well back in third.[22]) Not long before Finley Peter Dunne's column "On the Anglo-Saxon" appeared in the *Chicago Journal*, Frederick Jackson Turner had delivered his celebrated lecture at the Congress of Historians at the 1893 Chicago World's Fair on "The Significance of the Frontier in American History." The thrust of Turner's thesis, "a new paradigm for studying American history" as Martin Ridge puts it, was that the "colonization of the Great West" was the most powerful explanatory nexus of American institutions.[23] Turner, in effect, was suggesting the formation of a distinctively *American* polity. This in contradistinction to the "germ theory" of his professor, Herbert Baxter Adams, under whom he wrote his dissertation at Johns Hopkins University. (Note that Woodrow Wilson received his Ph.D. from Johns Hopkins in 1886, and was a visiting lecturer there 1888–98.) Adams, along with the generality of historians of his time, "believed that American institutions were primarily the result of their Germanic and Anglo-Saxon antecedents or 'germs.'"[24] Turner did not deny the European heritage, but argued that "[t]oo exclusive attention has been paid by institutional students of Germanic origins, too little to the American factors."[25]

Thus, while the American people knew themselves to be singularly various, American elites were offering up a mere three identities. We could be German, Anglo-Saxon, or American. Wilson *could* have kept us out of war, thereby hugely enhancing the notion of American isolation and exceptionalism. He *could* have sided with Germany in the emergent cause of anti-imperialism, espousing freedom for Ireland and India. The Germans, a decent, democratic folk, were actively supporting both these fine insurgencies, not least in the United States where there was much support for them. (Had not an enterprising Fenian, John P. Holland, invented the first true submarine, with which to sink the British merchant marine? In 1900, the U.S. Navy bought one, the U.S.S. Holland, from his firm which became the Electric Boat Company.) But no. Wilson, faithless to his campaign pledge to keep us out of war (or at least the pledge made in his name), took us *into* war to preserve the British Empire with its huddled masses on which never set the sun. He regarded American supporters of Irish independence, such as Daniel F. Cohalan, as little better than traitors. (And doubtless approved of the brief resurgence of the Loyal Orange Order which organized a considerable Twelfth of July parade in New York City in 1919. That being the anniversary of William of Orange's victory over the Irish Catholics at the Battle of the Boyne in 1690.) In 1918, his administration prosecuted twenty-nine Indian emigrés for conspiracy to violate the neutrality laws—neutrality, that is, in favor of the Raj—and sent fourteen to prison in the circumstances of traitors or as near as makes no matter. And why? I have pondered the subject for the better part of half a century and have reached no more satisfactory conclusion than that Woodrow Wilson, Scotch-Irish that he was, believed that Americans were of the "Anglo-Saxon race" and need come to the rescue of their brethren in Britain. Other cases can be made; this is mine.[26]

And so America, too, entered the Great War and the great darkness descended as the age of totalitarianism commenced. It took up most of the rest of the century; at mid-century, it was thought that it would never end. But then, of a sudden, it did. The visible breakup began early in 1989 and was over by the end of 1991.

Charles Krauthammer writes, "We have been privileged to witness miracles of biblical proportions,"[27] a phrase subsequently borrowed by President George Bush for his 1992 State of the Union address, amidst repeated invocation of a "new world order." The great trauma of totalitarianism ended. Rules returned to the international order; law even. Aggression in the Persian Gulf was defeated with the systematic employment of procedures set forth in the United Nations Charter. The principal powers seemed at long last to look to international organization and international law as normal, even necessary, institutions of the existing international order, which they now supported rather than challenged. Yet, with all this, the tumult of ethnicity, if anything, increased. The Soviet Union came apart along ethnic lines. The most important factor in this breakup was the disinclination of Slavic Ukraine to continue under a regime dominated by Slavic Russia. Yugoslavia came apart also, beginning with a brutal clash between Serbia and Croatia, here again "nations" with only the smallest differences in genealogy; with, indeed, practically a common language. Ethnic conflict does not require great differences; small will do. In late 1991, two rival Nigerian ethnic groups, the Tiv and Jukun, both primarily Christian, took to fighting over farmland. The resulting deaths in the thousands were barely reported in the West.[28] Deaths in the tens of thousands followed the escalation of civil war in 1991 between clans in Somalia, a country of some six million persons speaking the same language, most of them Sunni Muslims. Hawiye, Darod, Isaaks slaughtered one another as children starved. The world took note. The United Nations sent troops; the Red Cross sent food. The slaughter went on.

At the end of 1991, John Zametica of the International Institute for Strategic Studies in London described the Balkan stalemate as "a recipe for war without end."[29] The last 1991 issue of *The Economist* carried a survey of ongoing conflicts around the world under the heading, "Tribalism revisited." Yugoslavia served as the prototype:

> Yugoslavia has brought civil war back to Europe for the first time since Greece was rent in the 1940s and republican fought fascist in Spain in the 1930s. Yugoslavia's may well be the war of the future: one waged between different tribes, harbouring centuries-old grudges about language, religion and territory, and provoking bitterness for generations to come. In their details, conflicts like these vary from place to place. The tribes may want to dominate each other, to escape each other's clutches or merely to kill each other. But the main ingredient is the same: visceral hatred of the neighbours.[30]

By the spring of 1992, the breakup of Yugoslavia was manifest when Croatia, Slovenia, and Bosnia-Herzegovina were elected as full members of the United Nations. But fighting, if anything, grew worse. A new kind of war correspondent emerged, reporting massacres rather than battles. On May 24, John F. Burns of the *New York Times* filed this report from Zvornik in Bosnia and Herzegovina:

> The man's face was becoming tauter, and the screwdriver he was twisting in his hands turned ever more quickly while he

recalled his role in the recent ethnic killing. "It's difficult to explain," he said, as he sat in the hair salon on Zvornik's main street. "Normal people turn out to be beasts, as if you're watching a Frankenstein movie. They become monsters." In the dusk outside, nothing moved except the glowering Serb militiamen who are the town's new masters.

Anger, barely suppressed, erupting suddenly into violence; fear and suspicion fed by rumors and half-truths, becoming paranoia; a burning sense of past injustices unavenged, and of similar tragedies ahead, if ethnic rivals are not corralled, punished and expelled: This is Bosnia, six weeks into a civil war that is spiralling ever more dangerously out of control.

All of this in a republic of 4.4 million people that until this year seemed a model of what a multi-ethnic society in the Balkans could be. Until the Bosnian Serbs decided to contest the republic's secession from the Serbian-dominated rump of Yugoslavia, opting instead to use terror and forced expulsions to create "autonomous regions" purged of Muslim Slavs and Croats, many people who knew Bosnia said that if different ethnic groups could live together peacefully anywhere in the Balkans, it should be here.[31]

The disaster's roots, Burns continued, "seem to lie more in the realm of carefully inflicted psychological wounds than of current wrongs . . . ."[32] Two days later, a *New York Times* report was headed, "Winds of Yugoslavia's War Threaten to Engulf Ethnic Enclave in Serbia." Close to a million "ethnic Albanians"—our friends the Gegs living in Kosovo—had voted to secede from Serbia and become part of primarily Muslim Albania.[33] The term "ethnic cleansing" entered the language.

No one seemed to know what to do. If anything. The United States finally began to talk of economic sanctions, but mostly looked to Europe. Europe looked away.

William Pfaff went to the heart of the matter. "What
Serbia, and to a lesser extent Croatia," he wrote, "now
are doing in Bosnia-Herzegovina confounds [the] principle . . . that military aggression and the murderous
repression of ethnic minorities inside a state are matters
of international concern and will be challenged by the
international community."[34] An American State Department official allowed that this was a "dirty war . . . in
which people are murdered, tortured, not because of
what they do but because they belong to one ethnic
group or another."[35] In this instance, Muslims were the
most victimized. Pfaff noted that Islamic states were
asking whether world indignation over aggression seems
only to function when a Muslim state was the aggressor.
But China, a member of the Security Council, and other
Third World dictatorships feared that the principle of
international intervention might one day be turned
against *them*. Neither the United States nor the West
generally was prepared for any of this. As Pfaff had
known we would not be.

Others agreed. Writing in the *Chicago Tribune*, Ray
Moseley noted:

The current hand-wringing response to the murder of a
nation simply demonstrates the hollowness of the so-called
new world order that Bush envisaged after the Berlin Wall
tumbled and the former Soviet Union collapsed.

The new world order was never precisely defined, but in
general terms it referred to a world in which stability no longer
rested on the balance of power between competing military
blocs and in which problems were solved through cooperation
and the beneficent intervention of the U.S.

This formula for a Pax Americana overlooked the fact that
the breakdown of authority in the former Soviet bloc

unleashed nationalistic forces that had been bottled up for nearly 50 years in countries with fractious ethnic divisions. No mechanism was created or even envisaged for dealing with these conflicts, and America's seeming retreat from its world role is inconsistent with any attempt to maintain order in the world.[36]

In the meantime, the *New York Times* reported from Moscow: "Ethnic Battles Flaring in Former Soviet Fringe." Serge Schmemann wrote that the Nationality Question had not been resolved by the "stern 'socialist internationalism'" of the previous regime. To the contrary.

The roll call of warring nationalities invokes some forgotten primer on the warring tribes of the Dark Ages—Ossetians, Georgians, Abkhasians, Daghestanis, Azeris, Armenians, Moldovans, Russians, Ukrainians, Gaugauz, Tatars, Tajiks.

They die for lands much of the world has never heard of—Nakhichevan, Nagorno-Karabakh, the "Dniester Republic," South Ossetia—or for causes lost in the fog of history.

All along the southern fringe of the former Soviet empire, ethnic brush-fires that sprang up with the collapse of central authority have resisted all efforts at mediation and control. On the contrary, some now threaten to turn into major conflagrations, and new regions are beginning to smolder.

At a news conference this week, Marshal Yevgeny Shaposhnikov, the commander of the joint command of the Commonwealth of Independent States, created a stir when he warned that "if another side gets involved" in the Armenian-Azerbaijan fight, "we will be on the edge of World War III."[37]

The Marshal was alluding to Turkey, where public sentiment was

inflamed by the Armenian offensives in Nagorno-Karabakh, an

Armenian enclave in Azerbaijan, and Nakhichevan, an Azerbaijani enclave in Armenia. The Turks are closely related to the Azeris by language, culture and religion.

In recent weeks, Armenia has succeeded in driving the last Azeris from Nagorno-Karabakh and in breaking a corridor to it through Azeri territory. The Armenians have also shelled border areas of Nakhichevan.

Those attacks compounded Turkish resentments already fired by the well-publicized killings of civilian Azeris in Khodjaly, inside Nagorno-Karabakh, last February. The Turkish Government, however, has been keenly aware of the enormous dangers of getting directly involved, not least because of how Russia or the rest of the world might react, or what the consequences may be in expanding a conflict that pits Christians against Muslims.[38]

On May 25, Tass reported that the President of the former Soviet republic of Moldova warned of war with Russia if Russian troops continued to help Russian-speaking separatists in the Dniester region. The President Mircea Snegur stated, "The Moldovan Parliament has to choose between two decisions—either to stop military activities in the Dniester region, which is not possible in my opinion, or to declare that Moldova is in a state of war with Russia."[39] Elsewhere, it was reported that the Afghan freedom fighters, having taken Kabul, were now fighting among themselves along ethnic lines.[40]

The Economist of May 23, 1992, carried a table of "Displaced persons in ex-Yugoslavia as of May 12th." Some 1,205,000 according to the United Nations High Commissioner for Refugees. This estimate probably did not as yet include many Gegs, but then the Serbs could never be expected to give up the sacred field of the Grey Falcon where the Turks had prevailed in 1389.[41] A Geg leader had remarked of the Serbian President, former Communist, Slobodan Milosevic: "It's all a tragic absurdity. In fighting for Serbs in Croatia, and now in Bosnia and Herzegovina, [he] says that all Serbs have the right to live in a single Serbian state. But here in Kosovo, where Albanians would like to claim that right for themselves, we are told that we are not a nation, we are a minority. It's simply a matter of double standards."[42] *The Economist* was grim:

Because there was no need for tent cities to house the 600,000 registered refugees from Croatia, the scale of their suffering has impressed western television-watchers less than that of the Kurds in Iraq. That may be about to change. The war in Bosnia has doubled the number of refugees inside what was Yugoslavia. Tent cities are on their way.

In most wars refugees flee because of the fighting. In Croatia and Bosnia much of the fighting is designed to create refugees. Hitler talked of "resettling" Jews in his newly conquered eastern territories. In Bosnia and Croatia the phrase is "ethnic cleansing." It means that hundreds of thousands of people who happen to be of the wrong nationality in the wrong place (where their families have lived for centuries) must run for their lives.

How complacent were the generation of Europeans who grew up after the second world war thinking that such barbarous behaviour was something that happened nowadays only in unfortunate and far-away countries like Ethiopia and Bangladesh. Villages from which Serbs have fled in Croatia have been burned. Muslim villages in Serb areas of Bosnia are being burned to encourage their residents to leave. Croats in villages in Serbia are also being pressured to leave. Under the noses of United Nations peacekeepers, Croats in Serb-held territories of Croatia are being driven out. Serbs are fleeing towns in Bosnia where they are shot at, and towns in Croatia where they are frightened they will be. All sides have used massacre and mutilation to drive their messages home.[43]

And so I return to a subject I first took up far back in the 1950s when Nathan Glazer invited me to join him in a study of the ethnic groups of New York City, published in 1963 under the title, *Beyond the Melting Pot.* We managed to cover five such groups, which would come to about 3 percent of the current number of ethnic groups in the city. (In the three-year period, 1988–91, the New York Public Schools would enroll immigrant children from 167 different countries.) But we got to a large proposition, which was that ethnicity was very much a force in the polity, possibly stronger than it had been, such that it might even qualify as a *new* social aggregate, which would come to be known as post-industrial. Our conclusions were summed up in a passage that has made its way into "Social Science Quotations," volume 19 of the *International Encyclopedia of the Social Sciences.* "The notion that the intense and unprecedented mixture of ethnic and religious groups in American life was soon to blend into a homogenous end product has outlived its usefulness, and also its credibility. . . . The point about the melting pot. . . is that it did not happen."[44]

It is a liberty verging on license that I use the term "our" with respect to this passage. The essential insight was that of Glazer, who had started his journey, as you might say, writing *The Social Basis of American Communism,* which was published in 1961.[45] Of late I have taken to remarking that what Karl Marx wrote in the British Museum Glazer disproved in the New York Public Library, but that while you see, or used to see, statues of Marx all over the place, one hardly ever sees a statue of Nathan Glazer. Communism in America was largely an ethnic phenomenon. That having been established, the phenomenon of Marxism appeared in a wholly different light.

We were heard and yet not heard. Years later, as I will recount, I found myself in the United States Senate, as a member of the Select Committee on Intelligence, urgently, earnestly arguing the case that the Soviet Union would break up in the 1980s, and break up along ethnic lines. With a single exception, which I will also discuss, official Washington simply could not *hear* what I was saying. No one said I was wrong, it is simply that no one could pick up a signal sent on that frequency.

And so, it seemed to me useful to raise the subject in a setting such as that of the Cyril Foster Lecture. I more or less assumed we would not be intellectually ready for events such as now occur in what was Yugoslavia, to cite but one instance. We weren't. Nor for a moment do I think of ethnic conflict as something that happens elsewhere. *Beyond the Melting Pot* was an account of real, if contained, conflict. A third of a century later, the social condition of American cities is hugely deteriorated. We have just, as I write, suffered our worst urban riot in a half-century. A riot with a difference, new yet old. Asians were among the principal victims of violence against property. The current small-arms fighting in American cities is bound to escalate in terms both of weaponry and of aggression against whites; a role reversal, but the same drama.

We respond to all this with what Meg Greenfield has called "The Great Scott Syndrome," in which we are asked to believe that our leaders are "dumbstruck" by "the existence of a crisis in the cities."[46]

Commenting on the Los Angeles riot in the London *Independent*, William Rees-Mogg wrote:

Yet at present, the United States is unwinding strand by strand, rather like the Soviet Union, Yugoslavia or Northern Ireland. South Africa now seems to be the only rich country that is not moving towards a social, economic and ethnic apartheid. In 1992 the Los Angeles riots and the IRA bomb in the City of London—where 100 lbs. of Semtex did one billion pounds of damage—alike show the strength of the forces of disintegration and the vulnerability of our modern society to them.[47]

Forward-looking South Africa: a new thought. In any event, as they say, food for thought.

Hence, the title of my essay: *Pandaemonium*. The capital of hell in *Paradise Lost*. I came upon the reference in an almost elegiac essay by Solomon F. Bloom entitled, "The Peoples of my Home Town," which appeared in *Commentary* in 1947.[48] As I will discuss at greater length, Bloom describes his youth in a small market town in what was then Rumania. A place teeming with ethnicity, yet peaceable, synergistic, until the empires broke up and it all began to go wrong. Bloom describes how men, like Milton's demons, made themselves smaller "squeezing into Pandaemonium to listen to Satan."[49] If you will look for such passages elsewhere there are a surprising number. We may have handled these things better a century ago; two centuries ago. Is it possible we might learn to do better in the future? Are such things ever "learned"?

I do not know. All I know is that much of the present was foretold. In the autumn of 1972, Glazer and I convened a conference on ethnicity at the American Academy of Arts and Sciences. The proceedings began with a panel, "Toward a General Theory." Harold R. Isaacs presented a paper on "Basic Group Identity: The Idols of the Tribe." As later published, Isaac's paper put it thus:

We spin out as from a centrifuge, flying apart socially and politically, at the same time that enormous centripetal forces press us all into more and more of a single mass every year. World power is more concentrated and more diffused than ever before. . . . We have entered the postindustrial age before two thirds of the world has barely begun to emerge from the preindustrial era. . . . [50]

What then? Which is to say, what now?

CHAPTER 1

Ethnicity as a
Discipline

*I*T is no accident that ethnicity as a subject
has tended to be slighted, if not ignored. At the onset of
the twentieth century, there were two large ideas abroad,
curiously congruent, which predicted a steady or even
precipitous decline of ethnic attachments. Milton M.
Gordon has termed the first of these "the liberal
expectancy."[1] This is perhaps especially an American
view. Ethnic identities were seen as recessive, readily
explained by immigrant experience, but essentially transi-
tional. A proper "American" would emerge in time.
(Somewhere on the frontier?) Horowitz describes the
considerable ideological and intellectual lineage of this
"expectancy." Ethnicity is ascriptive, a consequence of
birth, which for Enlightenment political theorists "sig-
nified the chains of the feudal estates."[2] It was primitive.

That eminent Victorian, Sir Henry Sumner Maine, demonstrated that in primitive societies "kinship in blood is the sole possible ground of community in political functions."[3] By contrast, modern societies are territorial, a revolutionary innovation. Horowitz suggests that anthropologists are no longer so certain. In a nice turn: "the dialectical relationship between consanguinity and contiguity as organizing principles of community persists."[4]

Then there was the Marxist prediction. Ethnicity would give way to "proletarian internationalism," and that was that. Decreed. Folk-dancing might persist, even language differences, but these would be, in Stalin's celebrated phrase, "nationalist in form and socialist in content." Social class, an economic category, would be the all-determining crucible of identity.

The power of the Marxist decree may be seen in E. J. Hobsbawm's study, *Nations and Nationalism since 1780*, published in 1990. A work of great learning, it is equally a work of vast delusion. Not that the reader would suspect this from the jacket copy: "timely . . . succinct and masterly," is the verdict of *New Statesman*. Michael Foot, one-time leader of the British Labour Party, writing in the *Guardian*, declares: "[Hobsbawm] surveys the whole scene from the loftiest historical altitude but of course he never fails, great historian that he is, to supply the essential absorbing detail." (The volume, incidentally, is based on the Wiles Lectures given at the Queens University of Belfast, that peaceable kingdom.) Hobsbawm's singular conceit is the fact that nationalism is becoming a legitimate field of study somehow constitutes proof that this particular form of social relationship is soon to vanish. His closing passage: "After all, the very fact that historians are at least beginning to make some progress in the study and analysis of nations and nationalism suggests that, as so often, the phenomenon is past its peak. The owl of Minerva which brings wisdom, said Hegel, flies out at dusk. It is a good sign that it is now circling round nations and nationalism."[5]

None of this is to deny the salience of social class, or even to downgrade it. It is merely to assert that societies are more complex. It is now common for ethnic scholars to look at specific situations in terms both of ethnicity *and* class. Typically, class is measured on a horizontal axis, ethnicity on a vertical axis. In the simplest matrix, four groups emerge. Upper-class dominant ethnic group, lower-class dominant ethnic group, upper-class lower ethnic group, and finally, lower-class *and* lower ethnic group. This matrix was first employed by John Dollard of Yale in his classic, *Caste and Class in a Southern Town* (1937), a study of race relations in (as we now know) Indianola, Mississippi, in the early 1930s.[6] Dollard acknowledged that the *schema*—caste *and* class—was developed by W. L. Warner "and his group" at the University of Chicago, but as I wrote in a foreword to the fiftieth-anniversary edition of *Caste and Class*, they were made flesh in "Southern Town." Here was a system of hateful segregation and oppression—hateful at all events to the liberal outsider. But somehow internally stable. Dollard had discovered gains as well as losses incident to the caste and class arrangements, such that the arrangement, well, worked.

When Dollard died in 1980, there was little by way of obituary. I wrote a brief memoir for the *New York Times*

Book Review, in which I suggested that it was his peculiar fate to have so many of his ideas accepted during his lifetime that by the time of his death they were no longer associated with him. The most important of these is that the "usual human response to frustration is aggression." Previous to *Caste and Class*, and his later collaboration, *Frustration and Aggression*, American social science had pretty much settled on a utilitarian model in which behavior is explained by expectation of things yet to happen. Rewards or punishments. But here was a mode that reversed directions. Behaviour was to be explained in terms of events that had *already* happened. If you wished a child to behave, did you *give* him or her an ice cream cone? Or promise an ice cream cone? Complexity. Add that to the notion of caste and the world seems less perfectible a place. Caste, a given, can be a formidable source of frustration and, in varying circumstances and to varying degrees, of aggression. Dollard notes William Graham Sumner's observation that social class breaks down to people with habits. Habits change. But caste? Color? Creed? If ethnicity is seen as a form of caste, we commence to have a sense of its tenacity. Bearing ever in mind that the species is protean; people *change* color, creed, language. But categories persist.

As an instance of the caste and class composite, allow me to recount an episode in the East End of London in the year 1966. Harry McPherson (then Counsel to the President) and I happened to be in London at the same time and one evening went off to the East End with our wives for a tour of the public houses there. Toward the end of the evening, we found ourselves in a small pub on a side street. We were served our respective pints and accepted a friendly invitation to try our hand at darts. Our wives settled themselves on a bench set against the wall, with cockney ladies on either side. After two or three minutes scrutiny of the new dart players, the lady next to my wife pronounced: " 'E's Irish, 'e's Scotch; both Ni'vy." Which happened to be the case exactly.

Richard Hofstadter begins his canonical essay, "The Paranoid Style in American Politics," with the observation, "Although American political life has rarely been touched by the most acute varieties of class conflict, it has served again and again as an arena for uncommonly angry minds."[7] More often than not these minds have been angry about some issue of race or religion or nationality. But not *only* race. He notes that "[p]robably the most widely read contemporary book in the United States before *Uncle Tom's Cabin*" was Maria Monk's *Awful Disclosures*, an account of debauchery and worse in a Montreal nunnery.[8] Anti-Catholicism, specifically, belief in and fear of papist conspiracy, was at least as powerful an emotion in nineteenth-century America as was abolitionism. (Thus, Edwin M. Stanton, Secretary of War at the time, was quite convinced that Lincoln's assassination was the work of Catholic conspirators.) But the fading of these issues along with the emergence of a labor movement in the late nineteenth century, and the advent of socialist and Marxist parties (this latter largely the aftermath of immigration from central Europe) seemed to move American political life in the direction of class-based issues and organizations. By mid-twentieth century, the liberal expectancy and the Marxist prediction were all but unchallenged. Whereupon, Nathan Glazer and others began to challenge them.

In 1963, Glazer and I began our study, based on his design, *Beyond the Melting Pot: The Negroes, Puerto Ricans, Jews, Italians, and Irish of New York City.* As the title would indicate, our nominal concern was with the liberal expectancy. (The term "melting pot" as an image of the American immigrant experience was coined by the British playwright, Israel Zangwill. His play of that title depicts the triumph of true love in the New World over Christian–Jewish hostilities, specifically a pogrom in Polish Russia, brought over from the Old. Conveniently for our purpose, Zangwill in time became a Zionist, putting such assimilationism resolutely behind him.) A parallel concern, however, was the Marxist prediction, a matter of large moment in American intellectual circles. Glazer simply knew that Marx had been wrong; and that all that followed from Marx would go wrong. The book concluded on this note: "Religion and race define the next stage in the evolution of the American peoples. But the American nationality is still forming: its processes are mysterious, and the final form, if there is ever to be a final form, is as yet unknown."[9] Thirty years later this would seem as good a forecast as any; better than most.

Hence to a tentative point. The ethnic perspective can lay claim to some predictive power. Only some. But enough to warrant more respect than it has perhaps received. I deem it important that early on the most productive American scholars in the field were persons with some experience of Marxist thought, usually as members of a Marxist faction, or an *anti*-Marxist faction. Either way, they were much bound up with the strictures of proletarian internationalism, and alert enough to recognize a very different reality on the streets of, well, Brooklyn.

An example, verging on the prophetic, will be found in an obscure article, "Nationalism or Class?—Some Questions on the Potency of Political Symbols," which the then 28-year-old Daniel Bell published in *The Student Zionist*, a journal based at the University of Chicago, in 1947. This was one year before creation of the State of Israel. Discussing Palestine, be begins:

The basic political question in Palestine, apart from the immediate issue of immigration, is quite obviously the prospects of Arab-Jewish relations. The strategical policy of every Jewish political group is based on some perspective regarding the nature and direction of Arab thinking, ranging from the bi-nationalism of Hashomer Hatzair and Ichud to the violent Jewish particularism of the Irgun.

In the last analysis, each position is based on some estimation of the potency of certain symbols of identification. For the Hashomer, class consciousness in the Marxist sense is a strong enough cement to weld lower-class Arabs and working class Jews into a common front. For the Ichud, the liberal utopianism of peace and fellowship is of sufficient appeal to unite all men of good will. For the other Zionist groups to a lesser extent, and for the Revisionists to a greater extent, the emotions of nationalism are the most potent in creating group solidarity.[10]

The Hashomer Hatzair were, as Bell indicates, bi-nationalist Marxists: They looked to an Arab-Jewish worker state. The Ichud group, associated with Rabbi Judah Leon Magnes, chancellor and first president of the Hebrew University, were middle-class intellectuals and also bi-nationalists. What were the prospects of such a society? None, thought Bell. Not least because the Arabs were unlikely to "achieve that state of maturity which allows them to recognize a sense of class interest and rational cooperation with Jews."[11] Whereupon? Whereupon the idea of a *Jewish* state would prevail, and that Jewish state would seek alliances abroad: "If nationalism is still the key to political action, then a policy of national alliances may be necessary for survival. This would involve an effort toward closer affiliation with Great Britain or the United States."[12] This from a 28-year-old writing in 1947![13]

Getting on to a half-century has passed and ethnicity as a field of study has progressed. (Owing not least, of course, to Bell's formidable contributions, although his main interests turned elsewhere.) There is now, for example, a journal, *Ethnic and Racial Studies*, edited, significantly, by the London School of Economics. A scattering of scholars are beginning to claim some disciplinary status for a subject scarcely a generation old, at most incipiently quantitative, and rarely taught. A moment, in other words, that calls for audacity!

I will, accordingly, put the proposition that an ethnic perspective made it possible to forecast the break-up of the Soviet Union with some accuracy. But also, which is part of the story, with little hearing.

The great, commanding question confronting the democratic states in the second half of the twentieth century had to do with the destiny of the Soviet Union. Was it, in fact, as it proclaimed, the vanguard state of an international proletariat; the next stage in history; already on the scene; destined to prevail? Or was it possibly just the old Russian empire with a new vocabulary, jealous of status and prerogatives naturally enough, but capable of being lured toward *détente*, willing with time to settle into the scarcely ignoble status of a superpower, one of two?

Toward the end of the seventies, I had become convinced that neither scenario was credible. I did not think the Soviet Union or its ideas were going to inherit the earth. Nor did I think the Soviet Union was going to settle down to rule a large chunk of it. I thought the Soviet Union was going to break up.

In 1979 *Newsweek* magazine published a forum on "The Eighties." In a brief submission entitled, "Will Russia Blow Up?," I began: "The Soviet empire is coming under tremendous strain. It could blow up. The world could blow up with it."[14] This latter being a reference to the possibility of nuclear warfare— "loose nukes," as they would come to be known—between successor states drawn along ethnic boundaries.

Now this is not the language of an academic journal. Nor, clearly, was it entirely predictive. The Soviet Union did not blow up. It might have done had the old guard coup of August 1991 succeeded. But it did not, and in the end the U.S.S.R. mostly merely came apart. Nor was this fragmentation followed by nuclear war. Indeed, in 1992 the U.S. reached agreement with the four nuclear successor states, Russia, Ukraine, Belarus, and Kazakhstan, to abide by the terms of the Strategic Arms Reduction Treaty which had been negotiated in the 1980s. Over a seven-year period, all long-range nuclear warheads would be turned over to Russia and handled in accordance with the earlier agreement. It was declared that all tactical nuclear warheads—those which had concerned me—were already being turned over to Russia. Perhaps. It was not preposterous to raise the

possibility of an *internal* nuclear exchange. In any event,
I was writing in the context of a foreign policy debate of
vast importance. The United States was just then
entering a period when American foreign policy would
be hugely, if not decisively, influenced by a dissident view
from the right that the threat of Soviet communism had
grown greater than it had ever been. Containment was
seen to have failed; *détente* was seen to have failed; the
Soviets had launched a global offensive, holding the
N.A.T.O. front with new missiles whilst enveloping the
Third World flank. In time, the President of the United
States, Ronald Reagan, would note with alarm that
failure to aid the Nicaraguan *contras* would mean the
consolidation of a privileged sanctuary for terrorists and
subversives just two days' driving time from Harlingen,
Texas.[15]

I was by now a member of the United States Senate. I
had supported the increase in military spending that
began under President Jimmy Carter, but observed that
this in no way reassured, much less satisfied, the new
dissidents. They wished for a military posture approaching mobilization; they would create or invent whatever
crises were required to bring this about. To a considerable degree, for a time, they got what they wished
for. I watched all this with a mixture of incredulity,
horror, and complicity.

First the latter. I had come to the Senate from an
abbreviated posting, 1975–6, as United States Permanent Representative to the United Nations. I had
been sent there by President Gerald R. Ford at the behest
of his Secretary of State Henry A. Kissinger, after having
served as ambassador to India. My mission was to work

out an accommodation with the "non-aligned" majority in the General Assembly which had aligned itself with the Soviet Union and was making increasingly non-negotiable demands on the West for the transfer of resources and—crucially—the legitimization of an assertively anti-democratic Third World *dirigisme*. (Even India had succumbed to "emergency" rule.) Relations with the Soviet Union were seen to have stabilized, a *détente* having been achieved. Once at the U.N., however, I found things quite different. The non-aligned were in full throat, to be sure. But the Soviets were anything but the "satisfied power" that was supposed to have evolved.[16] To the contrary, they embarked on all manner of destabilizing initiatives and interventions. They master-minded General Assembly Resolution 3379, declaring that "Zionism is a form of racism and racial discrimination."[17] This put in jeopardy the very legitimacy and hence existence of a democratic state to which the United States had made the most profound commitments. When Portugal let go of Angola, the proclamation of the departing High Commissioner transferred power to the "Angolan" people rather than to any government. Predictably, there was no such thing. There were tribes with territories, notably the Bacongo in the north, the Kimbundu in the middle, and the Ovimbundu in the south of this vast region. The Kimbundu were organized in the Popular Movement for the Liberation of Angola (M.P.L.A.), a Marxist, pro-Moscow group, which controlled the capital. "Negotiations" broke down. The usual. When, of a sudden, in early October 1975, Cuban troops landed in the M.P.L.A. zone, followed by Soviet troops, pilots, and tank crews. *The*

U.S.S.R. had invaded Africa! As in time it would invade Afghanistan. Something *was* going on. In the event, I grew militant, asserting that the Soviets would not control the oil shipping lanes from the Persian Gulf to Europe and, in a flight of geo-political fancy, control a state "next to Brazil."[18] I became something of an embarrassment to my own government, and fairly soon left before I was fired. On my first day out of government, I joined the campaign of Senator Henry M. Jackson, then campaigning for the Democratic Presidential nomination. When this effort collapsed in Pennsylvania, I entered the New York Senate race, squeaked by the primary and was easily enough elected in the fall. In the Senate, I promptly aligned myself with Jackson and other Democrats who were of the view that even Republicans had grown soft on communism. I was made a member of the Senate Select Committee on Intelligence, and set out to prove the extent of the Present Danger, as it was referred to by a curious mix of activists and intellectuals, drawn largely from the left but now moving inexorably to the right. (More than a few Jackson Democrats would end up Reagan Republicans.)

I now began to change my mind. Little things at first. During my tenure at the United Nations, Arkady N. Shevchenko, Under-Secretary-General for Political and Security Council Affairs, defected to the United States. He was then the highest ranking Soviet in the Secretariat (an American has the matching position of Under-Secretary-General for General Assembly Affairs). An ambassador at 40, aide to Foreign Minister Andrei A. Gromyko, he was, as I have written elsewhere, on almost anyone's short list of those who might succeed

Gromyko. He was, in any event, the highest-ranking Soviet official ever to come over to our side in the course of the cold war. As his reward, in the pitiless mode of that Great Game, we kept him "in place". In time, Soviet intelligence realized the Americans had things we weren't supposed to have and by some process of elimination got to Shevchenko. *Not* before suspicions went right into the Kremlin itself. In 1978, they grabbed his wife, who committed suicide in Moscow, or so it was said. But Shevchenko got free, thanks in a large measure to the Federal Bureau of Investigation. He ended up in Washington, where we talked at length. He described in detail a police state in which political belief had all but leached out of the system. He himself had been just enough imbued with what he would call the ideals of the 1917 revolution that he could not bear the fact, obvious to him, that the state apparatus had no animating beliefs of any kind save the maintenance of power. He had nothing to gain by defecting; much to lose. But he could bear it no longer.

In a word, communism was dead. It would take time for this news to reach the Vietnamese jungle, Angolan bush, or Nicaraguan mountains. When an idea dies in Paris, or Lisbon, or Madrid, it is a generation, two generations before this is understood on the periphery. Fair enough. But I began to ask how it was that *we* seemed to have so little sense of this. Then there was the matter of the Soviet economy. For years I had listened to scientists such as Jack P. Ruina, head of the Defense Advanced Research Projects Agency in the Kennedy administration, ask if even the Soviets could be so cunning as to conceal a dynamic twenty-first-century economy behind the decrepit nineteenth-century façade which greeted visitors.

By this time, Murray Feshbach and Stephen Rapawy, both of the U.S. Bureau of the Census, had reported the sharp manpower shortages facing the Soviet Union. The growth rate of the workforce at the end of the century would be "about one-third the rate at the middle of the century."[19] Further (according to official Soviet statistics that their government soon ceased publishing), a difference of 10 years had appeared between the life expectancy of males and females at birth (64 years for males, 74 years for females). United Nations statistics indicated that "with the single exception of Gabon", there was no other country in the world in which such a wide gap was to be encountered.[20] This was 1976. Four years later, Feshbach and Christopher Davis of the University of Birmingham reported, "since 1971 the infant mortality rate has increased from 22.9 deaths per 1,000 live births to an estimated 31.1 per 1,000 in 1976."[21] The life expectancy at birth for Soviet men had now declined to 63 years, whilst that for women remained at 74 years. If demography is destiny, this was a society growing ill. Or, if you like, breaking down.

Finally, there was the matter of ethnicity. By the mid-1970s the demands of Soviet Jews to be allowed to emigrate had become a mass movement. Recall that this was the issue that evoked such savagery on the part of the U.S.S.R. at the United Nations. Why should they have commenced a massive, systematic effort to delegitimize the state of Israel, if not because a mass movement had formed within the Soviet Union to go there? A movement of persons defined by religious affiliation stamped on internal passports. If religion was alive among Jews, would it not be alive among Gentiles? If religion, then language; if language, then nationality. In short, there was no new Soviet man. (A fact Raymond Bauer had attested to at Harvard years earlier.)[22] All in all, a formula for instability.

A century hence there will be a considerable literature on the collapse of the Soviet "experiment." Milton M. Gordon cautions that there is a difference between the position that ethnic conflict overturned communism and the view that economic collapse allowed or induced ethnic tensions to surface, and that these have different implications for ethnic theory.[23] We are surely too close to the events, and as Westerners too distant, to have any definitive judgements.

Be that as it may, by the end of the 1970s, I had quite changed my mind. I had grown convinced that the danger from the Soviet Union would come not from its expansion, but its disintegration. Watching the economy decline, seeing the ethnic tensions rise, I came to the judgement—as a Senator and a member of the Select Committee on Intelligence—that the Soviet Union was about to break up.

The 1979 *Newsweek* article "Will Russia Blow Up?" continued:

[P]opulation in the Slavic republics has almost ceased to grow. Vitality at the center of the empire must be low indeed. Something happened. The moment came when it became clear that the promises of the revolution, especially the economic promises, were not being kept and would not be.

Now the nationality strains begin. Whatever Marxism may

have meant to intellectuals, it is ethnic identity that has stirred the masses of the twentieth century, and they are stirring near the Russian borders. John Paul II at the United Nations spoke to both these Soviet realities: that Soviet man is not free; that the Soviet peoples are enslaved.

Since 1920 the Communists have rather encouraged ethnic culture, while ruthlessly suppressing ethnic politics. It won't work. By the year 2000 one-third of the population will be Muslim. Less than half the population will be Great Russian. They will no longer be able to rule from the centre.[24]

I carried the argument to the Senate floor and elsewhere. Here is a sampling:

Senate Floor
January 10, 1980

[T]he Soviet Union is a seriously troubled, even sick society. The indices of economic stagnation and even decline are extraordinary. The indices of social disorder—social pathology is not too strong a term—are even more so. The defining event of the decade might well be the break-up of the Soviet Empire.[25]

New York University Commencement Address
May 24, 1984

The truth is that the Soviet idea is spent. It commands some influence in the world; and fear. But it summons no loyalty. History is moving away from it with astounding speed. I would not press the image, but it is as if the whole Marxist-Leninist ethos is hurtling off into a black hole in the Universe. . . .

If we must learn to live with military parity, let us keep all the more in mind that we have consolidated an overwhelming economic advantage. . . .

Our grand strategy should be to wait out the Soviet Union; its time is passing. . . . It will be clear that in the end, freedom did prevail.[26]

News Conference, Buffalo, New York
October 14, 1984

There is a basic fact, so elemental, why do we have difficulty understanding it: The Cold War is over. The West won. . . . The Soviet Union is a failed society and an unstable one. . . . The place has collapsed. As a society, it just doesn't work. Nobody believes in it any more.[27]

The Harper Dictionary of Modern Thought
submitted with Nathan Glazer, December 1986

In the *Communist Manifesto*, Marx and Engels forecast that all preindustrial distinctions of an ethnic character would disappear with the emergence of a world-wide industrial proletariat united by a perceived common condition and shared interest. The Workers of the World belief, central to Marxism, is increasingly presented as central to the falsification of Marxist prediction. . . . [28]

The New York Times
December 21, 1986

In a narrow but intensely active circle here [in Washington] there has emerged a consuming obsession with the expansion of Communism—which is not in fact going on. Something else is going on in places where we think we see a Communist threat: convulsive ethnic conflict. We seem to have no feel for that.

It appears to me that we have deeply misread events in the world. We have paid far too much attention to geopolitics and far too little attention to questions of political economy. . . .

The one enormous fact of the third quarter of the 20th century . . . is the near complete collapse of Marxism as an ideological force in the world. Nothing quite so sudden or so complete has ever happened. . . . We find a world convulsed with ethnic conflict that defeats any Marxist analysis.[29]

Senate Floor
October 2, 1987

Mr. President, in the course of . . . a decade in the Senate, I have spoken from time to time about what seems to me an essential event of this age: That the correlation of forces, if I can use that Soviet term, between the Soviet Union and the Western democracies has moved decisively against the Soviet Union, if not indeed against the whole of the Marxist world. . . .

No collapse has been more dramatic or more complete than this collapse of Marxist ideology.[30]

It may be useful to compare the predictive power of the ethnic perspective of the former Soviet Union with that of the "realist" perspective that attained such prestige in American diplomacy about half-way through the cold war. The Soviet Union was a fact; world communism was a fact. Hence, prepare for protracted conflict, perhaps with pauses of power-sharing. Thus, former President Richard Nixon, in his 1980 work, *The Real War*, on the durability of the Soviet threat:

Since [my resignation], the position of the United States relative to that of the Soviet Union has seriously worsened, and the peril to the West has greatly increased. . . .

During all of my presidency we were engaged in a "war" with the Soviet Union. That struggle with the Soviets will continue to dominate world events for the rest of this century. . . .

The danger facing the West during the balance of this century is . . . of drifting into a situation in which we find ourselves confronted with a choice between surrender and suicide—red or dead. That danger can still be averted, but the time in which we can avert it is rapidly running out.

The next two decades represent a time of maximum crisis for America and for the West, during which the fate of the world for generations to come may well be determined.[31]

ETHNICITY AS A DISCIPLINE

As to how durable President Nixon considered this threat, the book is dedicated: "To Our Grandchildren."

To say again, I pressed the contrary case. There was no response. None from the press. None from the Congress. None from the executive branch. Not even avuncular advice from the Directorate of Intelligence of the Central Intelligence Agency to lay off pronouncements that could only end with embarrassment. There is one exception to be noted because it is the *only*. In 1985, Max M. Kampelman became head of the U.S. Delegation to Negotiations on Nuclear and Space Arms, which met with the Soviets. I was one of a dozen or so Senate "observers" who would visit Geneva from time to time. Early on, Ambassador Kampelman had us to lunch, where in short order he asked if I would expand on the thought that the Soviets, with whom he was negotiating an incredibly complex superpower arms agreement, were in fact about to implode. I did, but to no consequence. It was simply not an idea in, if you like, our armamentarium. Kampelman would later write, "Whenever I am asked whether I had predicted the break up of the Soviet Union or knew anybody who did, I have uniformly stated that the one person who had fully understood and made the correct analysis was you."[32] But Kampelman, singularly among American public men, fits the profile earlier mentioned of ethnic scholars. Born in New York City. A research director for the International Ladies Garment Workers Union in a period when it was just emerging from an historic struggle with Marxist trade unionists more or less openly allied with the American Communist Party. Counsel in the Senate to Hubert H.

Humphrey, a survivor of not dissimilar struggles, and a public man who believed that ideas matter in politics. It will seem self-serving to cite Kampelman as I have done, but the tribute is intended for him. I may have been right or I may have been wrong: the point is that only he heard the argument being made.

This is no small matter. By mid-decade the United States government was, well, in the throes of a consuming obsession with an expansion of communism—*which was not happening.* The Reagan White House, with the active cooperation of the C.I.A. had claimed the Marxist regime in Nicaragua was shipping arms to Marxist guerrillas in El Salvador. This had been so, but was no longer. Even so it was a good enough excuse for mindless *apparatchiks* in the White House to put the Presidency in harm's way with the Iran-*contra* episode: All to gather funds with which to arm the opposition in Nicaragua. Theodore Draper would write: "If ever the constitutional democracy of the United States is overthrown, we now have a better idea of how this is likely to be done."[33] All this in the cause of fighting a cold war that was over!

In his retrospective collection, *The United States and the End of the Cold War,* John Lewis Gaddis tells of being invited early in 1985 by a Washington foreign policy institute to join a group of "experts" who would meet periodically to consider recommendations for American foreign policy toward the Soviet Union during the remainder of the decade. He accepted:

The meeting, as it turned out, was a disappointment. The participants seemed unable to focus on anything beyond the next few months, and their comments amounted to little more than reiterations of the need to continue existing policies. After listening to several hours of discussion along these lines, I very tentatively raised my hand and asked whether we should not be looking ahead to the possibility that the Cold War might someday end: should we not give at least some thought to how we would like it to do so, and to what might then replace it? An embarrassed silence ensued, broken finally by this observation from a highly respected senior diplomat: "Oh, it hadn't occurred to any of us that it ever would end."[34]

Seven years later, early in 1992, the Nixon Presidential Library held a conference in the same city of Washington to consider foreign policy in the aftermath of the cold war. The former President spoke, as did his former Secretary of State, Dr. Kissinger. In a morning session I gave a brief paper contending that the United States needed to look to its analytic abilities, given the failure of the executive branch to foresee the end of the cold war and the break-up of the Soviet Union, invoking some of the material cited here. In an afternoon address Dr. Kissinger was a touch acerbic, as the official transcript suggests.

The subject which I was asked to address was America's role in the new world order. As a student of history I can think of few examples, in fact I can think of no example where a nation achieved so completely what it set out to do as the United States has in the last two or three years. If one compares what the bipartisan leaders of the late '40s and early '50s were saying of the kind of earth that they wanted to bring about, it is almost exactly what has happened, except that nobody believed that it would happen so quickly. I know no one, at least I knew no one before this morning, who had predicted the evolution in the Soviet Union.

Now Mr. President, if you hold another conference a couple
of years from now and do me the honor of inviting me, I will
no doubt have convinced myself that I thought clearly at every
stage. (Laughter, followed by applause.) But at this point I
must say that while I had some belief of a disintegration of the
satellite orbit, it did not occur to me that we would see the
twin revolutions through which we are now living, the collapse
of Communism in the Soviet Union and the collapse of the
imperial system of the Russian empire.[35]

It must be recorded that there was other dissent from
the prevailing orthodoxy. In 1979, *Decline of an Empire:
The Soviet Socialist Republics in Revolt* by Hélène Carrère
d'Encausse offered an encyclopedic study of Soviet
ethnic groups. Marx, in her view, "seriously overes-
timated the part played by economic and social factors in
the development of nations," which had led to the
fantasy that a new Soviet man would emerge from the
Eurasian chaos.[36] She concluded:

Without question, the Kremlin is running into many problems.
But one thing is clear: of all the problems facing Moscow, the
most urgent and the most stubborn is the one raised by the
national minorities. And like the Empire that it succeeded, the
Soviet State seems incapable of extricating itself from the
nationality impasse.[37]

Again, little if any response.

In all, a cautionary tale for social science. On the one
hand, the economics profession egregiously overes-
timated the size and growth of, and was calamitously
mistaken about, the Soviet economy. Thus, in the mid-
1970s the C.I.A. had Soviet G.N.P. at 62 percent of U.S.
G.N.P.; later, East Germany ahead of West Germany in

per capita output.[38] These were consensus estimates among the allies and within the profession. Dale Jorgenson at Harvard has suggested that "this has to be one of the great failures of economics—right up there with the inability of economists . . . to find a remedy for the Great Depression of the 1930's."[39]

Just as significantly, Soviet studies by and large dismissed or ignored the ethnic dimension in assessing Soviet stability. Gaddis writes of the C.I.A., not without a measure of understatement: "It certainly failed to give sufficient attention to the survival of ethnic rivalries inside the U.S.S.R. and among its European satellites."[40] For what it is worth, ethnic studies are *said* to have been discouraged in the intelligence community as somehow "soft," even unscientific. But is it not possible to argue that had we been more understanding, more *analytical*, the cold war might have ended quite differently? Early in the 1980s, even as the prospect of Soviet disintegration became steadily more credible, it also became clear that the finances of the United States government were growing equally unstable. The Reagan administration had come to office determined to reduce the size of the Federal government by cutting its income. In the colloquialism of the time, to "starve the beast." Simultaneously, it wished to accelerate the defense build-up in the face of a new feverish concern with the Soviet threat. Taxes were cut, budgets were increased, and a huge deficit appeared. In time, President Reagan would more than moderate his views of the Soviet Union, but never understood the onset of fiscal instability. His first budget director David A. Stockman, who had hit upon the device for reducing the size of government, did in time come to see what he/they had done. He pleaded for new revenues. Was greeted with amiable incomprehension. He would write of this as "a willful act of ignorance and grotesque irresponsibility. In the entire twentieth-century fiscal history of the nation there has been nothing to rival it."[41] Commenting on this, Lou Cannon, who brilliantly reported the Reagan years for the *Washington Post*, was not much moved by young Stockman's conversion and subsequent anathematizing: "David Stockman's account of his days as President Reagan's budget director should be required reading for all ideologues who conspire by legal means to subvert, undermine or take over a democratic government."[42] Subversion. Again. And this, too, could be seen. At the time. Certainly by 1984 when I spoke of the impending crisis in an address to the Commonwealth Club of California that July. "As no political generation in history, ours may turn out to be one that squandered the nation's past, and paralyzed its future, and never noticed either."[43]

Surely, the cold war might have come to an end on its own without the U.S. having become a debtor state in the process. Had we seen what was coming, the West would have conducted its affairs differently. But, there it is. The Iron Law of Emulation took hold. Organizations in conflict become like one another.[44] The cold war establishment of the United States, as of N.A.T.O. generally, took the Soviets at their word. Their economy was booming and their society united. Dissenting economists, such as the Swede, Anders Åslund, who argued that the U.S.S.R. had at best a moderately advanced Third World economy, were either not heard or dismissed, while—to say again—the subject of ethnic disorder simply had no status in geo-political argument.[45]

George F. Kennan had seen that a policy of containment directed against Stalin's U.S.S.R. required, as he later wrote, "an adequate balance of opposing power, primarily political (because that was where the threat was) but also, in a defensive sense, military."[46] A routinized, apolitical intelligence community gradually lost sight of the primacy of politics. The time came when the political power of the Soviet Union had all but vanished from the international scene. Our intelligence community missed this altogether.

A former senior intelligence officer of the highest rank recalled Soviet defectors "who would tell us in anguished terms that the system was collapsing." No one listened, he recalls. "We had got into a routine of counting missiles. . . . [I]n 1987 there was not a single person in Washington who would have believed that the Berlin wall would come down in 1989. If I had suggested it might, instead of sending me off to a comfortable retirement they would have sent me to St. Elizabeth's."[47]

To the objection that the intelligence and defense communities need to be more than routinely aware of the "worst case scenario" there is the counter objection that this is precisely what was missed in the 1980s. Starting with the 1979 article I argued that as the system approached collapse the "wounded bear" might become more dangerous than ever. This argument made no visible impression. As we negotiated a strategic arms agreement (START) with an entity that would not exist by the time the treaty reached the Senate, I argued that another real danger was tactical nuclear exchanges between breakaway regions. Again, nothing.

If this is the case, then we have at hand a matter of some import. This would be especially the case if one further proposition proves true, namely, that totalitarianism was a one-time event in human history. Obviously, we do not and cannot know. To argue thus is to engage the work of a formidable body of American political science, as, for example, the work of Merle Fainsod, and, of course, some of the great classics of British literature from Huxley to Orwell. And yet, begin with William Pfaff's contention that Leninism merged into totalitarianism in part because it emerged from the surely one-time event of World War I. This is an extract from *On the Law of Nations*, the first indented passage being a direct quote:

> Whatever Leninism otherwise might have become, in the actual conditions of 1918 it took for its social model what was before it in the West—the war state, "totally" mobilized, with hundreds of millions of people under arms or drafted to war production, centrally planned, directed by governments given exceptional powers over how citizens lived, where they worked, how they died.

From the war on the Eastern front to the "war Communism" of the early Soviet state was a short walk indeed. Pfaff notes that Asian Communists shared this experience; Chou En-lai and Ho Chi Minh were in France at the time. Hitler was there, too. Carrying messages to the front, acquiring his wounds—psychic as well as physical—and learning firsthand how "total" war is waged.

Pfaff concludes that those who "accepted totalitarianism were in some sense retroactively justifying what they had been through in the world war. An appalling sacrifice had been demanded, and had been made. The values of the societies that enthusiastically had gone to war were the values that the war itself contradicted or discredited." Lenin, Chou, Ho, and Hitler adopted the methods, replacing the values. "Nihilism was thus the war's principal outcome."[48]

This question cannot be settled: it is enough for now merely to raise it. Basically, the argument must be that the values of which Pfaff speaks proved more enduring than anyone expected. Religious values, clearly. And civic. We may date the end of the cold war to the end of 1988 when Mikhail Gorbachev, General Secretary of the Communist Party of the Soviet Union, went before the General Assembly of the United Nations and declared: "Our ideal is a world community of states with political systems and foreign policies based on law."[49]

Totalitarian states remain; marginalized, but even so. The technology of social control if anything grows beyond the reach of even Orwell's imagining. The case is intelligently made that along with the atom the twentieth century bequeaths Big Brother to the centuries that will follow and there is no knowing when he might come up once more on the world screen. But that is yet to come, if ever. For the moment, Francis Fukuyama, in his celebrated essay, proclaimed "the end of history," asserting that the general tenets of liberal democracy were now unchallenged in the world and that matters would rest there.[50] And yet, there is a further fact attendant upon the end of the age of totalitarianism, which is the persistence of ethnicity. Attachments by no means necessarily liberal, never so irreligious as when pressed in the name of religion, restless and mutating all the time. This surely is where we must anticipate the violent clashes of communities and states in the years ahead. This is where it has arisen even during the age of totalitarianism. Fascism—Italian, then German—was much about "blood." The Second World War was as much pogrom as anything else, and far the greatest incidence of violence since has been ethnic in nature and in origin.

At one level the power of ethnic attachments, and ethnic conflict, can be explained in familiar enough terms. Years ago Ralf Dahrendorf noted that for the longest while—" 'from Locke to Lenin'—property dominated social and political thought: as a source of everything good or evil, as a principle to be retained or abolished."[51] And yet, he noted that in societies such as the Soviet Union, Yugoslavia, and Israel, where private property has been reduced to "virtual insignificance," social stratification persisted.

Ethnicity is in this sense a study of social stratification in modern, which is to say considerably "mixed up" societies. The papers presented at the 1972 American Academy conference were subsequently published under the title, *Ethnicity: Theory and Experience*. Glazer and I wrote an introduction. We were not recording any formal agreement, but tried to reflect a general disposition as follows:

[T]he new stratification is to a considerable extent correlated with ethnicity. It probably always was, but the preoccupation with property relations obscured ethnic ones, which, typically, were seen either as derivative of the former, or survivals from a precontractual age. Now, as Yugoslav Communists struggle hopelessly—or so it would seem—to achieve some equity of development and living standard as between Bosnia-Herzegovina, Croatia, Macedonia, Montenegro, Serbia, and Slovenia, as Israeli Socialists look with alarm at the persisting differences in the "social class status" of "European" Jews as against "Oriental" Jews in their homeland, as Great Russians prattle on about the equality of ethnic groups in the Soviet Union, while Ukrainians in Washington rally in protest at the *Russian* Embassy, and Jews in Moscow demand to be allowed to emigrate to Israel, it is *property* that begins to seem derivative, and ethnicity that seems to become a more fundamental source of stratification. Why is this? To repeat, our hypothesis is that ethnic groups bring different norms to bear on common circumstances with consequent different levels of success—hence *group* differences in status. This phenomenon is likely to be as much in evidence in an advanced capitalist society where property relations are attenuated, as in a Communist or Socialist society where they are abolished. A note of caution. As quantitative studies of these issues begin to provide data, they will certainly show that what is common to, say, all Yugoslavians, must be accorded much greater weight than what is disparate, but of this it may simply be said that the Croatians don't seem to know the "data."[52]

A perception which endures is that while ethnic attachments are surely pre-modern and universal, it is the *modern* state that seems most eager to *reward* ethnicity. This from the Introduction:

The strategic efficacy of ethnicity as a basis for asserting claims against government has its counterpart in the seeming ease whereby government employs ethnic categories as a basis for distributing its rewards. Nothing was more dramatic than the rise of this practice on the part of the American government in the 1960s, *at the very instant when such practice was declared abhorrent and illegal.* The Civil Rights Act of

1964 was the very embodiment of the liberal expectancy. "Race, color, religion, sex, national origin": all such ascriptive categories were *outlawed*. No one was to be classified in such primitive offensive terms. In particular, government was to become color blind. However, within hours of the enactment of the statute, in order to enforce it, the federal government, for the first time, began to require ever more detailed accountings of sub-groups of every description—job trainees, kindergarten children, kindergarten teachers, university faculties, front office secretaries—in terms of race, color, and sex. (We seem not yet to have proceeded to religion and national origin. And yet an application form of the Graduate Faculty of Arts and Sciences of Harvard University now states: "It is to your advantage to state if you are a member of an ethnic minority.")[53]

Daniel Bell had put the matter most succinctly: "Ethnicity has become more salient [than class] because it can combine an interest with an affective tie."

If these references seem contemporary to an American reader, as surely they will, then it may be we have a further suggestion of predictive power. The Yugoslavia references were my contribution to the first passage cited. In June, 1965, the U.N. had convened a "seminar" on the subject of Multinational Societies. The U.N. had acquired from the League an institutional aversion to the subject of "minorities." As its name itself suggested—United Nations—it seemed best to assume that all was behind us, that the world had settled down into nicely compact nation states. However, the subject was still at large, and in some circumstances which were never quite clear, the Yugoslavian government offered to play host to the gathering, choosing the magical setting of

Ljubljana in Slovenia. Typically, governments sent delegations headed by minorities. The British dispatched a Jewish peer and a Welsh M.P. The American State Department was not much interested, save for Harlan Cleveland, then an Assistant Secretary who was, as ever, ahead of the times. He asked if I would represent the United States (I was then an Assistant Secretary of Labor) and arranged for an omni-competent career diplomat, Martin Herz, then Counselor of our Embassy at Teheran, to accompany and watch over me. The papers presented at the seminar were in the main defensive, and in that sense of considerable interest. I returned to Washington to report that regardless of what we were told, the Serbs and Croats were going to fight one day.[54]

Let it further be recorded, then, that there was no disposition among this diverse group of academicians to *celebrate* ethnicity. American political and social science has been marked by a distinct wariness about human nature, if that term may be allowed. (For years Europeans asked: Why is there no socialist movement in the United States?[55] The answer may be that we knew better.) Ours was the first, and still probably the only, constitution which simply assumes that plunder is the preference of most men, aggrandizement in one form or another, and uses this as the activating force for the whole enterprise of government. "Theoretic politicians," as Madison put it, might go on about a Republic of Virtue.[56] Ours would assume anything but, but make a virtue of its absence. A "new science of politics" showed how this could be done, setting off one interest against another, one branch of government against another, in a system of checks and balances that would restrain behavior and make up, again in Madison's words, for "the defect of better motives."[57] This disposition may account for American openness to Freudian analysis, at least among social scientists. Dollard was also the first Freudian in American social science. In a later comment on *Caste and Class in a Southern Town*, he wrote: "I see man also as Freud saw him. If . . . Durkheim . . . sees man poised and timeless in the frieze of structure, Freud sees him the ambitious beast, shivering in the high wind of culture. Seen close, he smokes."[58]

This was a time, at mid-century, when there were great expectations for social movements based on the solidarity of oppressed, or merely lower-status, groups. But even then there was dissent. Gunnar Myrdal's *American Dilemma*, which appeared in 1945, was hugely, and importantly, optimistic about the future of race relations in the United States, but not in the least sanguine about some supposed solidarity of the wretched of the earth. "Our hypothesis is that in a society where there are broad social classes and, in addition, more minute distinctions and splits in the lower strata, *the lower class groups will to a great extent take care of keeping each other subdued*, thus relieving to that extent the higher classes of this otherwise painful task necessary to the monopolization of its power and advantages."[59]

Taking up this theme in his 1947 article, Daniel Bell argued in effect that lower-class groups will instinctively seek status gains by oppressing one another, rather than through some common assault on higher-status groups.

The utopian radical notion claims that it is "natural" for the oppressed to unite against the oppressors. But a dispassionate view of the American scene shows that the greatest store of hate against Negroes, the most oppressed group, lies among the poor whites. And this is not only true in the south, but almost equally so in the north. It is illusory to speak of discrimination as being practiced only by employers and landlords and to ignore the rampant resentments and suspicions among the working class against the Negro—and against the Jew.

We know that one of the strongest compulsions in our culture is the achievement of status—in a psychological sense, to gain recognition of the individual ego, of esteem of worth—of being a person. If one is not a person, distinguishable from others, then one cannot be a specific object of love. In that sense, there is a biological foundation for the need for status. If a man is part of the indistinguishable mass, no woman will pick him out as different from the others and worthy of specific affection. One of the strongest impulses in our culture is *emulation*, an imitation of those who have the highest status; this is the basis of fashions and other modes of social action. If, therefore, within a prestige system one is already on the lowest rungs of the ladder, receiving less regard than others, two paths are open: one, to unite with others and overthrow the bases of prestige; the other, to search about and find some person or object at whose expense one can gain prestige. The first is a long-range interest with little guarantee of success; the second, of shorter range, with a greater probability of success.

Of what we know of human frustration and displacement, aggression rather than love is likely to be the course.[60]

Bell distinguished between "positional goods" and "distributional goods." The former are always in short supply, and are most readily acquired through ethnic organization. (Indeed, class solidarity of the socialist tradition is all but hostile to positional goods. Here and there, the early British Labour Party, say, there has been an attempt to define the working class in terms of near-ethnic *élan*, with a distinctive dress, speech, manners. But in the main, cloth caps do not the chieftain make.) In Bell's world view, Freud would ever prevail over Marx.

Freud once remarked that we pass from group psychology to individual psychology. The former is prior not only in historical but in psychological time as well. The first and basic group is the family. In political terms, the first unit was the tribe, because it was built on the basis of family. With the disintegration of the tribe other dependency structures appeared. Nationalism is potent because it recapitulates psychologically the family structure. There is authority for protection and there is identification and warmth. Where one seeks to pose class against nationalism, the failure to find elements of pride on the part of class allegiance is a strong handicap. Sometimes messianic hope can substitute for pride, as it did among the European working class. In large part today, that hope is forlorn. Where class appeal is united with nationalism, directing the antiplutocratic feeling against a national outsider, as Hitler did, the result is the creation of an internally cohesive movement.[61]

In a paper written for the 1972 conference, Bell, in particular, was at pains to distance himself from any celebration of ethnicity. He located the power of ethnicity partly as a device for making group claims on resources, something Madison would have understood, but also in the emotional rewards of love—and hate. Bell quotes Freud in *Civilization and its Discontents*: "*Homo homini lupus.* Who, in the face of all his experience of life and of history, will have the courage to dispute this assertion? . . . It is always possible to bind together a considerable number of people in love, so long as there are other people left over to receive the manifestations of their aggressiveness."[62] And he concludes:

I would like to sound a note of normative caution on the role of ethnicity in politics. The upsurge of ethnicity is a cultural gain in that it allows individuals whose identities have been submerged, or whose status has been denigrated, to assert a sense of pride in what they regard as their own. In equal measure, it is a means for disadvantaged groups to claim a set of rights and privileges which the existing power structures have denied them. Yet if one looks down the dark ravines of history, one sees that men in social groups need some other group to hate. The strength of a primordial attachment is that emotional cohesion derives not only from some inner "consciousness of kind," but from some external definition of an adversary as well. Where there are *Gemeinde*, there are also *Fremde*. And such divisions, when translated into politics, become, like a civil war, *politique a l'outrance*. It was once hoped that the politics of ideology might be replaced by the politics of civility, in which men would learn to live in negotiated peace. To replace the politics of ideology with the politics of ethnicity might only be the continuation of war by other means. And those are the drawbacks of ethnicity as well.[63]

That said, there remains, as Horowitz insists, a need for a theory to explain ethnic conflict, as well as a policy for ameliorating it. He makes the enormous contribution of distinguishing between ranked and unranked ethnic systems. On the one hand, there is Hierarchical Ordering of Ranked Groups corresponding to Weber's use of "caste structure." Group A dominates Group B, and this is understood by all, often accepted by all. There can, of course, be more than two groups in such a hierarchy. On the other hand, there is a Parallel Ordering of Unranked Groups. Hutu and Tutsi in Burundi, Protestant and Catholic in the Netherlands. In the former, class coincides with ethnicity. There are thus two variants: "situations in which class coincides with ethnicity and those where it cross-cuts it. In the former, one needn't preempt the other, because ethnic warfare equals class warfare (Burundi). In the latter, ethnicity is the more compelling affiliation, as family is more compelling than workplace . . . ."[64] The term *polydomainal* has been applied to such later groups, which are at least marginally less conflict prone. Alternatively, more easily separated![65] The question is in any event more than absorbing. It is compelling for the simple reason that the global conflicts of the twentieth century have produced the international norm that one and all are entitled to something called self-determination.

CHAPTER 2

On the "Self-Determination of Peoples"

HE 1972 conference on ethnicity of the American Academy of Arts and Sciences brought together a considerable range of academicians who found much in common in what had previously seemed isolated study. Isaacs's "Basic Group Identity: The Idols of the Tribe," was touched with alarm, or at least urgency. Isaacs, then teaching at the Massachusetts Institute of Technology, fitted well into the company. Jewish, and it would appear a former Trotskyite, much a man of the world in the sense that he saw events in world terms. He did not deplore ethnicity. To the contrary, he saw it as primordial, building on the work of Erik Erikson, who,

in turn, began with Freud, who had written that his sense of "identity" as a Jew resulted from "many obscure emotional forces which were the more powerful the less they could be expressed in words . . . . " Isaacs continues (citing Erikson):

The actual German words used by Freud, Erikson stresses, can hardly convey in English translation the depth of their usage. Here, he says, Freud is speaking of identity "in a most central ethnic sense," suggesting "a deep commonality known only to those who shared in it, and only expressible in words more mythical than conceptual." Identity, he says here, "is a process 'located' *in the core of the individual* and yet also *in the core of his communal culture*, a process which establishes, in fact, the identity of these two identities."[1]

Isaacs emphasizes the psychological role which group identity plays: "I believe it is possible to say that in all cases the *function* of basic group identity has to do most crucially with two key ingredients in every individual's personality and life experience: his sense of *belongingness* and the quality of his *self-esteem*."[2] In his conference paper:

An individual belongs to his basic group in the deepest and most literal sense that here he is not alone, which is what all but a very few human beings most fear to be. He is not only not alone . . . he cannot be denied or rejected. . . . It is home in the sense of Robert Frost's line, the place where, when you've got to go there, they've got to take you in.[3]

Alongside these powerful psychological factors Gordon hypothesizes a low-level biological disposition to ethnocentrism that varies in intensity by individuals and social circumstances, and is exacerbated by class or caste structures that keep groups apart. He agrees that ethnic group identity becomes incorporated into the sense of self and that "the passions and intensity of intergroup relations tend . . . to reflect the passions and intensity of individual interaction in those cases where crucial issues of ego-defense are at stake."[4] There is nothing beyond hypothesis in either view: but hypothesis is where you begin.

Isaacs feared, at times even dreaded, what he felt was now to come. "We are experiencing on a massively universal scale a convulsive ingathering of people in their numberless groupings of kinds—tribal, racial, linguistic, religious, national."[5] This phenomenon followed the collapse of the great empires in 1918 and 1945 and the "breakdown or inadequacy of all the larger coherences or systems of power and social organization."[6] The old "larger coherences" have not been replaced: "What we are experiencing . . . is not the shaping of new coherences but the world breaking into its bits and pieces, bursting like big and little stars from exploding galaxies . . . each one straining to hold its own small separate pieces from spinning off in their turn."[7]

Neither of the two superpowers had been able to replace the old empires: "both found the globe disconcertingly unmanageable."[8] The Soviet Union, in particular, was to find coping with the problem of ethnicity impossible. The Bolsheviks had promised national autonomy and territorial separateness, but:

These promises were broken, precisely on the rock of the "national question," which never ceased to be a central issue in Communist theory and a very live issue in Communist politics.

Almost involuntarily from the beginning and then deliberately under Stalin, Russia became a national-Communist power. It subverted revolutionary movements elsewhere to its own national strategic goals and policies. . . .

Neither visionary beliefs, then, nor large-scale industrialization and urbanization, nor the passage of generations, nor concentrated centralized power, nor massive repression, nor elaborate theories, nor structural schemes have apparently been able to check the survival and the persistence of the distinctive separateness of the many nationalities or tribes of people who live under the Communist system.[9]

From which it followed that in time, the tribes would demand self-determination. It was, after all, their right; enshrined in the United Nations Charter. Article 1 of the Charter sets forth "The Purposes of the United Nations." These are, Section 1, to "maintain international peace and security," and Section 2, to ensure "friendly relations among nations based on respect for the principles of equal rights and self-determination . . . . " That it might not be possible to do both things at one time seems hardly to have occurred to the drafters of the Charter. Nor, as we will see, was the matter allowed to detain them.

The dilemma, if it is that, was graphically displayed in the Persian Gulf War of 1991. The Iraqi invasion of Kuwait the previous year produced an unprecedented international response. As never before in history, international law was invoked and international organization in the United Nations Security Council set about its putative task of applying the U.N. Charter.

However, the moment Iraqi forces were expelled from Kuwait ethnic divisions within Iraq itself broke out into civil strife.[10] Shi'ite Moslems rose against the Sunni authorities in Baghdad and slaughter commenced in southern regions, including Karbalah, where Shi'ism began with the defeat and death of Husain, the Prophet's grandson, in A.D. 680. In the north ethnic Kurds rose once again, and were once again driven into the mountains and across borders into Turkey and Iran, from whence they were driven back amidst great suffering. Now, however, the international community did not seem to know just what to do with its new found solidarity and activism. Resolution 688 (1991) was adopted stating that the Security Council:

1. *Condemns* the repression of the Iraqi civilian population in many parts of Iraq, including most recently in Kurdish populated areas, the consequences of which threaten international peace and security in the region.[11]

In this context the French began to talk about a "right of intervention" arising from general principles of humanitarian law. Mario Bettati, professor of international law and former dean of the Law School, Université de Paris-Sud, wrote that "By passing Resolution 688 on April 5 [1991], the United Nations Security Council broke new ground in international law, for the first time approving the right to interfere on humanitarian grounds in the hitherto sacrosanct internal affairs of member states."[12] In fact, the Security Council found a way to subsume the particularism of internal ethnic conflict with the universalism of the Charter's rules concerning breaches to international peace. Although Article 2(7) states emphatically that "Nothing contained in the present Charter shall authorize the United Nations to intervene in matters which are essentially within the domestic jurisdiction of any state," the Security Council determined that the massive flow of Kurdish refugees over Iraq's borders and into Turkey and Iran had created a "threat to the peace" and, therefore, justified further action by the Council under Chapter VII of the Charter. And, indeed, American and British forces were deployed in parts of Kurdistan, so called, along with U.N. relief workers. And yet when it was all over, Iraq was still in Saddam's control.

The Kurds were calling for self-determination. They did not get it this time around, any more than in previous efforts. But no one should suppose they will not try again. For are they not entitled to it under Article 1, Section 2 of the Charter? And is it not the case that in the period now in prospect, this will be the most troubled of international questions? It will not be as important perhaps as shifts in wealth and patterns of trade, nor yet of weapons development and diffusion, but it will be involved with both—especially the latter—and it will be troubled.

It is fitting enough that the United States, which is likely to bear much of the international tasks attendant upon the right of self-determination, is the state that first asserted this right, and the first to bring it to international councils. This occurred at the outset of the twentieth century, when we could still think of ourselves as a former colony that had gained independence in this manner and wished well to all those others who might also wish to do so. This was the work of Woodrow Wilson, and as I have said before, no man before and none since has ever attained to the international renown that Wilson experienced in the fateful months, extending to a year perhaps, following World War I.

For all that we were siding with two distinctly imperial powers, Wilson took us into that war in the name of self-determination. There is no historical problem concerning the origins of the doctrine. It begins, as Donald Cameron Watt of the University of London records, as the right of the subject of a state to choose their own government, that celebrated assertion of the American Declaration of Independence of 1776, followed by the French Declaration of the Rights of Man in 1789.

From this, by way of the nationalist assumption that the state must reflect the national group, self-determination came to encompass additionally the idea of national groups seceding from multinational states and empires in order to set up their own national state. As such it played an important part in Allied propaganda during World Wars I and II (e.g. in the FOURTEEN POINTS), was embodied at various points in the Charter of UNO, and became the main basis for anti-IMPERIALISM.[13]

As with any general assertion, the devil is in the details. Dr. Johnson got it just right when he asked in 1775: "How is it that we hear the loudest yelps for liberty among the drivers of Negroes?"[14] So much for Thomas Jefferson. So much as well for Woodrow Wilson, who was attended by slaves during his Virginia youth, and whilst the greatest friend of freedom for the Azerbaijanis of the world, sent a segregated American army to Europe to fight for such freedom. And had it not been segregated when he came to the Presidency, he would have seen to the matter before he left. For the devil of ethnic division is usually up and about. As if to ward off the evil, the United States early on took as its motto, *E pluribus unum*, from an early poem of Virgil describing, as John Augustine Wilstach put it, the nice touches of Italian cuisine. As his nineteenth-century commentary explains:

The lines are laudatory of early habits and rustic poverty. They close with a description of the ingredients and mode of preparation of a salad composed of garlic, parsley, rue, and onions, seasoned with cheese, salt, coriander, and vinegar, and finally sprinkled with oil. . . .

So that we may say, with probable truth, that, in describing an Italian salad, a frugal shepherd of the Roman Republic dictated that motto [*E pluribus unum*] which has served as the symbol of union for States in a hemisphere then unknown, for a Republic which uses, with enthusiasm, even the language of that illustrious government to which it is indebted, under so many forms, for safe precedents and wise examples.[15]

For, of course, that union almost came apart in a disastrous civil war over slavery in which one section of the United States asserted the right of self-determination, and the central government mounted the first modern industrial war in order to deny it that right.

That should have taught a lesson; it did not. The lesson that minorities not infrequently seek self-determination for themselves in order to deny it to others. *Homo homini lupus.* The dissolution of the Soviet Union was peaceable enough in the Slavic regions; at least, in the early stages of what will be a half-century or more process. As noted, the Caucasus region was not so fortunate. In early 1992, a bulletin by Serge Schmemann of the *New York Times*, dateline Moscow, began: "The latest communal atrocities in the former Soviet Union have again thrown the spotlight on the conflict in . . . . "[16] Fill in the blank.

By that time the spotlight was beginning to focus on whether the Russian Republic could even hold itself together. On March 31, 1992 Boris Yeltsin signed a treaty with eighteen of the semi-autonomous regions of the Russian Republic, granting to each "the right to 'independently participate' in foreign relations and foreign economic affairs, to govern itself based on its own constitution and laws and to choose its own anthem, flag and state symbol."[17] Even then Chechenya and Tatarstan, both oil-rich areas, refused to sign.

What are the dimensions of this issue? Merely to ask provides an answer of sorts. Which is that there is no answer. There are, for example, few clear answers on the subject in international law, despite rulings from the International Court of Justice on Namibia and Western Sahara. The U.N. exists to "develop friendly relations among nations based on the principle of . . . self-determination of peoples . . . . " What is a people? The Charter doesn't say. Nor does any other international agreement. A kind of negative definition is possible. The idea of self-determination arose in the context of demands for independence from rulers whose authority came down to the proposition that in some legal sense they ultimately owned the land. The time came when this in itself did not provide sufficient legitimacy to repel claims based on various kinship ties. "The principle is generally assumed to apply to people of the same 'nation' or 'nationality.' "[18] Language is the commonly asserted bond, and thanks to the prodigious exertions of the

Summer Institute of Linguistics of Dallas, Texas, we can estimate there are 6,170 languages spoken in the world at this time.[19] Which suggests the enormous potential for growth in the membership in the General Assembly. In 1985, Connor estimated that nearly half the then-independent countries in the world had in recent years experienced some degree of ethnically inspired dissonance.[20] He counted just seven homogeneous states with no border problems—Denmark, Iceland, Japan, Luxembourg, the Netherlands, Norway, and Portugal, accounting in all for less than 4 percent of the world's population. He notes further that leaving out Japan leaves us with less than one percent of the world's population. That same year Horowitz described a general pattern of less advanced groups attacking more advanced groups.[21] The issues are generally described as those of inequality, but the sources of inequality and its forms are seemingly infinite. Horowitz's pattern would be predicted by Dahrendorf's 1961 lecture, "On the Origin of Inequality among Men" at the University of Tübingen.[22] There *is* something called social science!

As to immediate prospects, we can begin at the beginning with the Balkans. The end of Yugoslavia came quickly enough, but not before considerable fighting, sometimes described as the first general war in Europe since 1945. As for central Europe, Hungarian opinion was openly irredentist during the latter years of Marxist rule. (In 1956 Joseph Cardinal Mindszenty sought sanctuary in the American embassy in Budapest, where he remained for fifteen years. He is remembered there as much for his bitterness toward Woodrow Wilson and the Versailles Peace Treaty as for his anti-communism.) The tectonic plates of the Commonwealth of Independent States will be grinding away for the foreseeable future. Southeast Asia is the scene of endless ethnic tension and increasing violence. Both Jawaharlal Nehru's daughter and his grandson were assassinated by ethnic separatists of one or another kind. This process, if such a term is appropriate, has now begun on the Horn of Africa with the proclaimed independence of Eritrea from Ethiopia. The post-colonial leaders of Africa quickly settled on a rule that none would challenge the colonial boundaries they inherited from the Conference of Berlin or whatever. This was an act of prescient statecraft, but not likely to endure. Western Europe has a familiar range of separatist movements, as does North America. These are handled with greater or lesser degrees of skill. Just now, for example, the United States government is caught up with the seemingly intractable problem of resolving the status of Puerto Rico, a prize of colonial war taken from Spain in 1898. At the United Nations we have insisted that Puerto Ricans are free to choose between statehood (which is to say membership in the American union), the present Commonwealth status, and independence. However, despite the urging of President Bush that Congress provide for a referendum which will enable the citizens of Puerto Rico to make such a choice, Congress has not been willing to do so. Congressional resistance arises largely from the question of whether the island should have the option to choose statehood whilst retaining Spanish as an official language. In two centuries, the United States Congress has admitted thirty-seven new states to the original union of thirteen. But always a stated or unstated condition was that English be the official language. Louisiana, for example, might and did retain the *Code Napoléon*, but trials were to be in English. This position may seem arbitrary, but it is defensible. *E pluribus unum*. But arbitrary or not, it can be predicted that Congress will remain seized of the issue, and the plebiscite delayed, for the simple reason that it suits the purposes of certain of the contending Puerto Rican parties *not* to have a plebiscite on terms which they perceive they would lose.

This tactic was to be seen in August 1991, when the Special Committee on the Situation with Regard to the Implementation of the Declaration on the Granting of Independence to Colonial Countries and Peoples (!) of the U.N. General Assembly adopted a resolution:

> *Deploring* the fact that the United States Congress has not yet adopted the legal framework for the holding of a referendum to enable the people of Puerto Rico to determine their political future through the exercise of their right to self-determination,
>
> *Recognizing* that the Legislative Assembly and the Governor of Puerto Rico, in the exercise of their powers, have approved legislation declaring Spanish to be the official language,
>
> *Hoping* that the international community will continue to afford Puerto Rico the opportunity to participate in those international activities which correspond to its political status . . .

The avowed object of this resolution is to encourage Congress to pass legislation providing for a plebescite. Almost certainly, however, the actual objective was to make this impossible by insisting that "Spanish . . . be the official language." The United States Congress has never

ON THE "SELF-DETERMINATION OF PEOPLES"

accepted the idea of a state with an official language other than English. (There is in fact no official language in the United States, although one state, California, has recently declared English to be the official language of California. Still, to provide for a language other than English is probably beyond the reach of the political realm at this time.) The incumbent administration in San Juan supports Commonwealth status, the current legal arrangement first established in 1952, although this was but dimly if at all perceived on the mainland. The Commonwealth party, led by a large figure, Luis Munoz Marin, did not see this new status as a way-station on the path to statehood. It would be more accurate to say that its members thought that it was the nearest thing to independence that could be realistically hoped for. Hence, the Puerto Rican Olympic teams and such like "international activities" referred to in the U.N. resolution.[23] In the meantime, however, opinion in the United States moved toward a fairly easy acceptance of statehood; this, for example, being President Bush's preference. Hawaii, Alaska: Why not Puerto Rico? Also in the meantime there has been an enormous expansion of Federally mandated, uniform welfare benefits. The dollar amount of these benefits is roughly related to median income levels in the United States, but in Puerto Rico such benefits would place otherwise dependent persons high in the upper half of the income distribution. This in turn has brought increasing support for the nominally Republican statehood party from the natural supporters of the vigorously Democratic Commonwealth party, giving the latter an understandable disinclination to pursue the rites of self-determination. This and other

aspects of the subject were raised by witnesses at the
U.N. hearing, as reported by the *San Juan Star.*

Several civil rights groups also testified, criticizing U.S.
repression and persecution of independence supporters and
evidence of colonialism and urging the release of so-called
Puerto Rican political prisoners in U.S. jails.

Civil liberties attorney William Kunstler, representing the
Puerto Rico subcommittee of the National Lawyers Guild,
questioned why the United Nations was quick to act to oppose
Iraq's invasion of Kuwait but slow to pressure Washington for
self-determination on an island invaded by the United States
nearly 100 years ago.

"There seems to be one standard for Saddam Hussein and
another for Bush and company," Kunstler said.

Two witnesses representing separate independence struggles
joined the Puerto Rico hearings to draw attention to their
causes, the Alaskan independence movement and the Brehon
Law Society linked to Northern Ireland.

Alaska's delegate warned that statehood increases depen-
dence on the United States, suggesting the U.N. place Alaska
again on the list of U.S. colonies.

Attorney Jeanne Bishop of the Brehon Law Society compared the British occupation of Northern Ireland to U.S.
occupation of Puerto Rico, urging decolonization in both
sites.[24]

It should be recorded, however, that the final vote in
the full Committee was only nine in favor, with one
against, ten states abstaining, three were recorded as Not
Voting, and two as Absent. There were then still a
handful of more or less self-confident tyrannies in the
world—Cuba, Syria, Iraq—pleased to record their disdain for the United States. A catatonic, imprudent
U.S.S.R. joined them. But Yugoslavia stayed out of it, as

did China. Self-determination was waning as an issue which Marxist regimes deployed as a technique to embarrass and, where possible, weaken democratic states.

Establishing self-determination as a norm of international law was an American project, and as with many American projects, it is a fine amalgam of idealism and self-interest. Americans are frequently distressed to learn of the self-interest part; those abroad are just as frequently dismayed to learn of the idealism. It is our condition and we can do no other. It is possible, even so, to disentangle some of the patterns, enough so as to attempt some assessment of present prospects.

The O.E.D. traces the lineage of the term self-determination to the celebrated 1911 edition of Encyclopaedia Britannica, "A Dictionary of Arts, Sciences, Literature and General Information"—still, at that time, a British publication. The article on Rome, by Henry Francis Pelham and Henry Stuart Jones, records that in the imperial period "the more enlightened of the emperors—especially Hadrian—made a genuine endeavour to give a due share in the work of government to the various subject races. But nothing could compensate for the lack of self-determination . . . . "[25] This is serendipitous at the very least, for it was precisely in the context of world empires that the issue arose six or seven years later.

Freud was evidently of the Lamarckian persuasion and held that the anxiety he discerned among late nineteenth-century Europeans was an acquired characteristic dating back to the onset of the Ice Age. It is not necessary to be anything so determinist to judge that twentieth-century western societies are at most just now beginning to recover from the shock of the First World War, and the dismantling of European empires, including the Ottoman Empire, that continues to this day. The war had not run its course before the promise of independent statehood to minorities, as they were now being called, became a tactic whereby one side sought to weaken the other. There is a certain poignancy in the second use of "self-determination" recorded by the O.E.D. On December 28, 1917, the West learned the terms the central powers were offering the Russians in the East. At Brest-Litovsk (typically, even the site of the peace conference had both a German and a Slavic name), Count Czernin, Austro-Hungarian foreign minister, offered what he almost certainly thought to be reasonable terms on behalf of the "Allied (Teutonic) Powers." (Czernin strove mightily for an early peace.) In a brief document, Clause 3 stated it to be the view of the Powers that issues concerning "those nationalities who have no political independence cannot . . . be solved internationally."[26] But next: "Clause 4. Likewise, in accordance with the declaration of statesmen of the Quadruple Alliance, the protection of the rights of minorities constitutes an essential component part of the constitutional rights of peoples to self-determination. The Allied Governments also grant validity to this principle everywhere, in so far as it is practically realizable."[27]

Too late. Six weeks later, on February 11, 1918, Woodrow Wilson would proclaim the same principle for the *other* alliance, albeit without notable consultation with the other allies. He told a cheering Joint Session of Congress: "National aspirations must be respected;

peoples may now be dominated and governed only by their own consent. 'Self-determination' is not a mere phrase. It is an imperative principle of action, which statesmen will henceforth ignore at their peril."[28] Some years later Winston Churchill would write that the idea was "neither original nor new" and that indeed the "phrase itself is Fichte's '*Selbst bestimmung*' ". Still, he judged, " 'Self-determination' will rightly be forever connected with the name of President Wilson."[29] The phrase does not appear in the celebrated Fourteen Points address to Congress a month earlier on January 8, in which Wilson set forth principles for a peace settlement. However, six of the Fourteen Points concerned what he would soon call self-determination.

8. Evacuation of German troops from all French territory and the return of Alsace-Lorraine to France.

9. Readjustment of Italian frontiers along clearly recognizable lines of nationality.

10. Limited self-government for the peoples of Austria-Hungary.

11. Evacuation of German troops from Romania, Serbia, and Montenegro, and independence guaranteed for the Balkan countries.

12. Independence for Turkey, but an opportunity to develop self-government for other nationalities under Turkish rule, and guarantees that the Dardanelles be permanently opened as a free passage to ships of all nations.

13. Independence for Poland.

As a war-fighting technique, it worked. Arthur S. Link writes that the speech, filled with other equal or higher ideals, undermined German morale during the final months of the war and "also gave the Germans a basis upon which to appeal for peace."[30]

That and more. *Twenty* years later in a speech in Berlin, Adolf Hitler made his "last territorial demand." The state of Czechoslovakia had been created in the name of self-determination. But the Peace Conference had botched the job. Minorities were oppressed in the new state. No matter: "[A]t last, nearly twenty years after the declarations of President Wilson, the right of self-determination for these 3,500,000 [Germans] must be enforced."[31]

As with the history of the age, so with the history of the idea. Self-determination makes its way from the enlightenment of the eighteenth century to the darkness of the twentieth. Americans do not hesitate to take credit for the idea. Forty years, thirty for sure, of contumely from the representatives in the General Assembly of former colonies has not *quite* quenched our ardor. As the Soviet imperium broke up, or continued to break up, in 1991 Karl E. Meyer evoked Wilson's Joint Session speech in the *New York Times*:

If one were to choose the man of the hour in post-Communist Europe, his name might well be Woodrow Wilson, long deceased and seldom celebrated. For he was the President who memorably informed Congress in 1918 that "self-determination is not a mere phrase. It is an imperative principle of action . . . "

From the Baltics to the Adriatic, from the Ukraine to the Balkans, oppressed millions have given new life to his imperative—and often troublesome—principle. Indeed, if results are the measure, Wilson has proved a more successful revolutionary than Lenin. . . .

Wilson, who died defeated and embittered, has earned the epitaph bestowed by Londoners on Sir Christopher Wren: If you wish to see his monument, just look around.[32]

Well, yes. And, no. Wilson did not create nationalism, nothing of the sort. But did respond to it with the doctrine of self-determination. At the level of statecraft, that is his. Absent him, the "principle" of self-determination would not be ratified by the United Nations Charter; it was he who put it on the agenda of international order. It is a monument in more than one sense.

Meyer acknowledges that Wilson's achievement has not been nearly so harmonious and sanctified as St. Paul's Cathedral. Indeed, Wilson's Secretary of State, Robert Lansing, thought the phrase was "simply loaded with dynamite" and presciently—Meyer's term—foretold the trouble to come. Lansing's Confidential Diaries, now in the Library of Congress, have never been published. It is in the interests of American diplomacy that they be better known, for a realism comes through that is not always prominent in our pronouncements. We are now in Paris, at the Peace Conference. Here are entries from December 20 and December 30, 1918, written in a fastidious hand with topics printed in block letters in the upper right-hand corner of the pages:

CERTAIN PHRASES OF THE
PRESIDENT CONTAIN THE
SEEDS OF TROUBLE

December 20, 1918

There are certain phrases in the President's "Fourteen Points" which I am sure will cause trouble in the future because their meaning and application have not been thought out. The principal ones, as I see them today, are those which declare that open covenants between nations should be "openly arrived at", that in imposing government over people they should have the right of "self-determination", and that there should be "freedom of the seas". These three phrases sound well and will obtain popular applause but each one contains the seeds of discord. . . .

When the President talks of "self-determination", what unit has he in mind? Does he mean a race, a territorial area or a community? Without a definite unit, which is practical, application of this principle is dangerous to peace and stability. . . .

These phrases will certainly come home to roost and cause much vexation. The President is a phrase-maker par excellence. He admires trite sayings and revels in formulating them. But when he comes to their practical application he is so vague that their worth may well be doubted. He apparently never thought out in advance where they would lead or how they would be interpreted by others. In fact he does not seem to care so that his words sound well. The gift of clever phrasing may be a curse unless the phrases are put to the test of sound, practical application before being uttered.[33]

It was at this time in Paris that Walter Lippmann, who assisted Wilson in preparing the Fourteen Points, wrote of Colonel House that "His advice is sought . . . because it is believed to be a little nearer this world than the President's and a good deal nearer heaven than that of Lloyd George . . . . "[34] But House could do little to ease Lansing's doubts. Wilson was determined. If Europeans were wary, they went along for what it might bring them in other matters. At this time, for example, Léon Bourgeois, head of the committee drafting the French proposals for a League of Nations, was insisting on an international army, the better to fight the Germans next time.[35] The Japanese wanted a clause in the treaty about racial equality. That was somehow out of the question. But up to a point, whatever Wilson wanted was fine, even if his advisors knew better. Again, the Secretary of State:

"SELF-DETERMINATION"

AND THE DANGERS

December 30, 1918

The more I think about the President's declaration as to the right of "self-determination", the more convinced I am of the danger of putting such ideas into the minds of certain races. It is bound to be the basis of impossible demands on the Peace Congress, and create trouble in many lands. . . .

The phrase is simply loaded with dynamite. It will raise hopes which can never be realized. It will, I fear, cost thousands of lives. In the end it is bound to be discredited, to be called the dream of an idealist who failed to realize the danger until too late to check those who attempt to put the principle into force. What a calamity that the phrase was ever uttered! What misery it will cause! Think of the feelings of the author when he counts the dead who died because he coined a phrase! A man, who is a leader of public thought, should beware of intemperate or undigested declarations. He is responsible for the consequences.[36]

Lansing was a lawyer, an *international* lawyer. He had been a founder of the American Society of International Law (1906) and helped establish the American Journal of International Law (1907). His *Notes on Sovereignty from the Standpoint of the State and the World* is a work of jurisprudence that no other Secretary of State in this century could have attempted, much less carried off. He had no great faith in international organization, however, and was quick to spot generalities that could collapse into unmanageable particulars. Perhaps as importantly, and just as singularly, he had been a Democratic county chairman in upstate New York. This is a particular *genus.* Upstate New York Democrats were at that time, and remain to this day, a minority in a solidly Republican region of the state. Just as importantly, it is a party of sometime minorities, Irish-Catholic, French-Canadian (Jefferson County borders the St. Lawrence River), with a few "old" families of Jeffersonian persuasion. The Lansings, neighbors to the Dulleses, were of the latter group. It was the custom of Woodrow Wilson, as of Franklin D. Roosevelt, to have Irish-Catholics get him elected and then disdain them for the not always edifying practices involved. Lansing had presumedly seen such practices up close. He knew about minorities and about grievances. Of all such, there was none with a greater constituency within Wilson's Democratic party, and within the United States electorate, than that of the Irish. On June 6, with the Peace Conference well underway, the Senate passed a resolution expressing "its sympathy with the aspirations of the Irish people for a government of their own choice."[37] In Paris on June 11, Wilson received a delegation of Irish-Americans, including Frank P. Walsh, who had been a member of the National War Labor Board. We have it from his later testimony before the Foreign Relations Committee that he reminded the President of his declaration of the right of self-determina-tion—words which "voiced the aspirations of countless millions of people." To which Wilson, who could not get the British to admit any "Irish" representatives to the conference, and probably didn't much try, replied, again in Walsh's recounting:

> You have touched on the great metaphysical tragedy of to-day. . . . When I gave utterance to those words I said them without the knowledge that nationalities existed, which are coming to us day after day. Of course, Ireland's case, from the point of view of population, from the point of view of the struggle it has made, from the point of interest that it has excited in the world, and especially among our own people, whom I am anxious to serve, is the oustanding case of a small nationality. You do not know and can not appreciate the anxieties that I have experienced as the result of these many millions of people having their hopes raised by what I have said.[38]

Walsh can be taken as a reliable, if not disinterested, *rapporteur*. We may conclude then that by June of 1919 Wilson had begun to share Lansing's forebodings about self-determination. Again, "too late." The standard had been raised for all the world to rally to, and in this sense, the course of the twentieth century was set.

Lansing spoke from practical experience; that of a lawyer and a party official. There was another view abroad in the United States at this time which also found the idea of self-determination theoretically suspect. This was the critique of capitalism and imperialism that found its political outlet in assorted socialist parties. As much a mass movement as an intellectual tendency, it opposed war; always had done, and when this war came it was crushed. Eugene V. Debs ran for President in 1912 and received 900,369 votes. Wilson put him in jail. The first American Red scare now began. There is a poignant note

on the page of the *New York Times* which carried the text
of Czernin's peace terms at Brest-Litovsk. A brief
account of a meeting in Manhattan of the Intercollegiate
Socialist Society recorded the presence of Norman
Angell, later Sir Norman, and other luminaries including
Dr. Frank Bohn and Frederic C. Howe. The story
concludes:

> Mr. Bohn, who said he heard recently through secret
> channels from Karl Liebknecht, the minority Socialist in prison
> in Germany for his anti-Kaiser views, declared that Liebknecht
> sent this message to America: "The war must not stop until the
> Emperor is overthrown." He declared the policy of Postmaster
> General Burleson in suppressing radical newspapers to be
> "idiotic."
> Unless the minorities make their voice felt, they will wake up
> in five years and find that the peace congress at the end of the
> war was similar to the Vienna Congress, which did not
> represent the "budding aspirations of the people," said Mr.
> Angell.
> Industrial life ought to be so organized that there would be
> no surplus wealth to exploit and cause wars, was the
> contribution of Mr. Howe.[39]

Angell would go on to become a Labour Member of
Parliament, a knight, a winner of the Nobel Peace Prize
for 1933.[40] But Liebknecht, having gone over to the
Communists under Rosa Luxemburg, would be assas-
sinated by proto-fascists in Berlin in 1919. Life for
American socialists was nothing so severe. President
Harding let Debs out of jail and had him over to lunch.
But they were painted with the broadbrush of the Red
scare, and then systematically shoved aside by the real
thing. Still, the disposition is worth recording.

Few serve this purpose as well as Thorstein Veblen. Economist, intellectual, rebel, professor. In 1917 he published a dense volume, *An Inquiry into the Nature of Peace and the Terms of its Perpetuation*, picking up from Kant's essay, *Zum ewigen Frieden*. He begins by arguing, in effect, that there is a patriotic gene: not quite your selfish gene of modern theory, but hereditary withal. There is, in any event, this somewhat confusing passage:

The patriotic animus appears to be an enduring trait of human nature, an ancient heritage that has stood over unshorn from time immemorial, under the Mendelian rule of the stability of racial types. It is archaic, not amenable to elimination or enduring suppression, and apparently not appreciably to be mitigated by reflection, education, experience or selective breeding.

Throughout the historical period, and presumably through an incalculable period of the unrecorded past, patriotic manslaughter has consistently been weeding out of each successive generation of men the most patriotic among them; with the net result that the level of patriotic ardor today appears to be no lower than it ever was. At the same time, with the advance of population, of culture and of the industrial arts, patriotism has grown increasingly disserviceable; and it is to all appearance as ubiquitous and as powerful as ever, and is held in as high esteem.

The continued prevalence of this archaic animus among the modern peoples, as well as the fact that it is universally placed high among the virtues, must be taken to argue that it is, in its elements, an hereditary trait, of the nature of an inborn impulsive propensity, rather than a product of habituation.[41]

No Lamarckian *he*. While it is not entirely clear whether he is being sardonic, his basic point is that the trait which may once have been serviceable to the "hybrid stock" of Christendom, no longer was.

Veblen was evidently invited to submit such thoughts as he might have to the Inquiry, the celebrated seminar that Wilson in the fall of 1917 had requested Colonel House to get started in order to be ready when peace came. He submitted two papers, which were called "Suggestions Touching the Working Program of an Inquiry into the Terms of Peace" and "An Outline of a Policy for the Control of the 'Economic Penetration' of Backward Countries and of Foreign Investments."[42] The first proposed a League of the Pacific Peoples, alternately, the Pacific League. Visionary though he may have been, Veblen simply assumed that in order to keep the peace an international organization had to be made up of mature industrial democracies.

[I]n the projected League the substantial core would be constituted, at the outset, by the chief democratic belligerents . . . ; admission being free to any others possessed of the necessary qualifications. The second class or group of peoples under the League's jurisdiction—those who would answer to the Territories in the American scheme—would be made up, in the main, of nationalities which are now under German, Austrian, Bulgarian or Turkish rule; to be held under surveillance, on probation, with so much of self-direction in their administrative affairs as the circumstances would admit, and with a view to their presently coming into standing as qualified members of the democratic federation of peoples. The third and outlying group, the wards of the League, would comprise those characteristically backward peoples that inhabit Colonial Possessions. By grace of fortune, the greater proportion of these pronouncedly backward peoples have now come under the hands of those nations who will presumably exercise the discretion in laying down the lines of the Pacific League's economic policy.[43]

As for nationalities, Veblen was for getting rid of them.

Within the confines of the League, it is evident, a sane policy looking to the perpetuation of the peace at large, should consistently incline to discard, or at least to disregard, distinctions of nationality, so far as the sentimental preconceptions of its constituent peoples will allow. The most fortunate outcome of this point would be the total obsolescence or obliteration of national demarcations. . . .

Their place and functions as political or civil units would then be supplied by a neutral scheme of administrative divisions, drawn without regard to present political frontiers and with an eye single to administrative convenience, as determined by the natural—topographical, climatic, or linguistic—parcelment of the countries to be taken care of.

The nationalities so drawn into the scheme of redistricting need not be disturbed in any other respect than that of their civil and political powers. They would cease to have any civil status, but their integrity or solidarity in the cultural and sentimental respect would be left undisturbed and, indeed, legally unnoticed; very much as is now formally the case with various minor nationalities in some parts of the Balkans and the Russian dominions; or, again, the Armenian nation; or the Jews in the English-speaking countries.[44]

The Armenians of this time would have been pleased to learn that they had been "left undisturbed." Looking back, it seems clear enough that no one had thought through, no one could have thought through the specifics of restoring stability in the aftermath of so much convulsion. The League of Nations was effortlessly undone by fascist and communist powers whose purposes were anything but pacific. The United Nations was almost instantly paralyzed by the veto given to the totalitarian Soviet Union. At least it can be said for the League that it expelled most of the members intent on war. And it can be said for the United Nations that a great war never did come, and in time the Soviet regime imploded. But looking about for modes of successful international cooperation there is no equivalent to the European Community as fashioned by profoundly practical men such as Jean Monnet, and yet envisioned, it could be said, by the likes of Thorstein Veblen, the least practical of men.

And so we record that there were those about in 1917 and 1918 who were concerned that self-determination would prove as unstable a principle in world affairs as had the previous imperial systems which so obviously had clashed in Central Europe. Thus, the imperial governments outside Central Europe, those not yet stricken by much the same forces, resisted introducing the doctrine of self-determination into their affairs.

The term did not make its way into the Covenant of the League. Lloyd George was not about to preside over the dismantling of the British Empire; that would be the work of others.[45] It was to apply to the realms of the defeated empires: the Hohenzollerns, the Hapsburgs, the Ottomans. Here we come upon a kind of time warp. The British and American leaders of the First World War and the peace that followed were quite prepared to use self-determination as a war-fighting strategy, and equally prepared to apply the principle with honest intent in devising a peace settlement in Central Europe. But they, notably the British, had not at all divested themselves of the notion that *they* could rule over subject peoples, and could add to them. This was an earlier mindset that continued in place alongside a new sensibility that in time would make the old one seem bizarre if not outright culpable.

It was there in the Fourteen Points:

5. Free, open-minded, and absolutely impartial adjustment of all colonial claims.

Clearly, this referred to claims by one colonial power on another colonial power to rule over assorted peoples not much to be consulted in the matter. The idea of conquest fair and square had not disappeared from the Western mind. Nor yet, as we have seen, from the ruler of the Third Reich bent on self-determination and more for an invented Aryan people.[46]

Presently, war resumed. A civil war in Western civilization which would display both the unities and divisions of that civilization. James M. McPherson has noted that in the American civil war the armies of the North and South rallied with equal fervor to the same hymn, "The Battle Cry of Freedom." So it was with self-determination in the Second World War. First self-determination for the German peoples, then self-determination for those the Germans had conquered in the name of self-determination, then . . . .

Now it was America's turn not just to propose terms, but to impose them. The President of the United States was Franklin D. Roosevelt. In the vast literature of this presidency, Roosevelt's connection with Wilson is rarely touched upon, giving rise to a reasonable doubt as to whether the Roosevelt historians have fully absorbed it.[47] He was in fact a dedicated Wilsonian. In 1918 and 1919 as Assistant Secretary of the Navy, he had worked to preserve the Treaty and the League as few other members of the official family had, certainly as no other member of the subcabinet.[48] The "Former Naval Person," which is to say former Assistant Secretary of the Navy, had in fact met Churchill in 1918 and was a bit put out that the former First Lord of the Admiralty did not later recall this. If anything, this stirred Roosevelt's Wilsonianism.

In her admirable study, *A History of the United Nations Charter*, Ruth Russell begins the discussion of self-determination with Wilson's various initiatives.

Although the United States had rejected Woodrow Wilson's ideas on international organization after the First World War, Americans widely approved his concept of self-determination and in the course of time extended its application to all colonial peoples. . . . American leaders, including the President, were convinced that the demands for self-government and independence by colonial peoples were destined to be a major political factor in the postwar world. . . . Self-determination, in American eyes, was part of the Atlantic Charter and a recognized postwar aim.[49]

Much as in the case of the Fourteen Points, the term self-determination does not appear in the actual text of the Charter agreed to at the Roosevelt-Churchill meeting off the coast of Newfoundland in August 1941. But the spirit was there in the "common principles" on which they would base their hopes for a better world. "[T]hey respect the right of all peoples to choose the form of government under which they will live; and they wish to see sovereign rights and self-government restored to those who have been forcibly deprived of them."[50]

Once again we see a war aim at work. The United States is about to enter on the side of Great Britain. In 1917 it was facing defeat; in 1941 it was facing conquest. At both moments the British ruled the world's largest empire. The United States government, while pro-British, was anti-imperialist. In the end, nothing too explicit is put on paper, but the sum of it is wholly different from anything in the past.[51] The most powerful states in the world, in combination that is, declare that "power" politics are at an end, that the world should be organized along lines of legitimacy deriving from the will of the peoples involved. History changed. The fact was that the British had now avowed principles which held the seeds of inevitable destruction for their empire, as the ubiquitous Evelyn Waugh noted in *A Tourist in Africa*: "ironically enough, the British Empire is being dissolved on . . . principles which we ourselves imported, of nineteenth-century Liberalism. The foundations of Empire are often occasions of woe; their dismemberment, always."[52]

Once again the Soviet Union proved to be the willing instrument of history. The Charter of the United Nations was signed on June 26, 1945, in San Francisco, at the conclusion of the United Nations Conference on International Organizations which had convened the previous April. Early on, the Soviet Union proposed to amend "the somewhat innocuous statement of the second purpose of the Organization," as Ruth Russell has it, in the Dumbarton Oaks draft with the italicized words: "To develop friendly relations among nations *based on respect for the principle of equal rights and self-determination of peoples*, and to take other appropriate measures to strengthen universal peace." Russell sums up:

The United States delegation felt that the Soviet proposal could be used as a cover for Soviet expansionism, but agreed that it would be difficult to oppose the principle.

The insertion was accepted by the four foreign ministers and thereby became a sponsors' amendment, without any discussion or interpretation being noted in the American records. Afterwards, however, Foreign Minister Molotov declared in a press conference that the Soviet Union "attached first-rate importance" to the newly added principles of "equality and the self-determination of nations." These goals would "draw [the] particular attention of the populations of colonies and mandated territories," which would help to realize them sooner. "We must first of all see to it," he commented, "that dependent countries are enabled as soon as possible to take the path of national independence." This should be promoted by the United Nations, which must act to expedite "the realization of the principles of equality and self-determination of nations." The Soviet view, at any rate, was left in no doubt.[53]

And there it ended. Or rather began. A drafting subcommittee poked at the subject for a bit. The French member asked what self-determination meant. The Briton averred that he was reluctant to encourage a discussion that would get nowhere. In a footnote, Russell records the denouement: "The Soviet member . . . suggested asking the Ukrainian chairman for the opinion of Committee I/1 on the exact meaning of self-determination. When asked, 'Mr. Manuilsky thought that the right of self-determination meant that a people may establish any regime which they may favor.' "[54]

The drafting went forward. The Soviet language was also included in Article 55, which begins Chapter IX on INTERNATIONAL ECONOMIC AND SOCIAL COOPERATION. Chapter XI was given the title DECLARATION REGARDING NON-SELF-GOVERNING TERRITORIES, which effectively declared an end to empire in the Western mode:

Members of the United Nations which have or assume responsibilities for the administration of territories whose peoples have not yet attained a full measure of self-government recognize the principle that the interests of the inhabitants of these territories are paramount, and accept as a sacred trust the obligation to promote to the utmost, within the system of international peace and security established by the present Charter, the well-being of the inhabitants of these territories, and, to this end:

a. to ensure, with due respect for the culture of the peoples concerned, their political, economic, social, and educational advancement, their just treatment, and their protection against abuses;

b. to develop self-government, to take due account of the political aspirations of the peoples, and to assist them in the progressive development of their free political institutions, according to the particular circumstances of each territory and its peoples and their varying stages of advancement . . .

There were moments of dissent, in the manner of Lansing. The drafting subcommittee that did not draft but simply adopted the initial provision on self-determination, did have the gumption to note that "an essential element of the principle in question is a free and genuine expression of the will of the people, which avoids cases of the alleged expression of the popular will, such as those used for their own ends by Germany and Italy in later years."[55] When it came to the DECLARATION REGARDING NON-SELF-GOVERNING TERRITORIES, a British delegate brought up some home truths:

[I]t was only the existence of our African Colonial Empire, and the essential materials which we could draw from it and the reinforcement route to the Middle East across the heart of Africa, it was only these which saved us from defeat. And if we had been defeated at that time, very likely none of us would be sitting here today. . . . Throughout this war the essential products of these territories and the use of bases . . . were available not only to ourselves, but to all the United Nations. . . . And the same is true of the French territories which rallied to General de Gaulle and of the Belgian Colonial Empire. Those colonial empires in fact were welded into one vast machine for the defence of liberty. Could we really contemplate as the conscious aim of our deliberations, the destruction of this machine or its separation into its component parts? That, Mr. Chairman, would indeed be a strange result of this Conference. Do not let us rule out independence as the ultimate destiny of some of these territories. . . . But to have included it as the universal goal of colonial policy would, we believe, be unrealistic and prejudicial to peace and security.[56]

Last in this regard came Chapter XII, INTERNATIONAL TRUSTEESHIP SYSTEM. The future had already arrived in San Francisco. Or was it the past? Peace had no more returned than the French sent troops to Syria and Lebanon, much in the mode of 1918. But where Zionists and Arabs had pretty much got along at Paris in 1918, now there was bad blood all round. The new United Nations would take over the old Mandates of the League of Nations, with Palestine more troubled than ever. The Soviets wished to include the term "self-determination"—their term now—in Article 76 on the "basic objectives of the trusteeship system." The British and French asked if the Russians wanted civil war in Palestine. Possibly they did; probably. In the end the article called for "progressive development towards self-government or independence," which it was agreed came to much the same thing.[57]

And so another new world order came into being. In one sense the Westphalian state system was finished. The United Nations began with fifty members; by mid-1992 there were 178. (About a third of the total membership is represented by former British possessions.) George Will, a wonderfully perceptive American commentator, observes that, "The most powerful idea of the modern age is that of culturally distinct people finding fulfillment in nationhood, often the revival of ancient nations."[58] America let loose this idea upon the world and it is now pretty much what the world thinks.

It has to be insisted, however, that this is a surpassingly fuzzy idea. There is no satisfactory answer to the question as to what self-determination, as more or less guaranteed by the U.N. Charter, actually *means.* In response it could be asked: What did all those Americans yelping about liberty in 1776 mean by the term? But that question had an answer. The courts of the time could tell you well enough what liberty was. For the citizen, at very least, the courts could recognize the deprivation of liberty. There was a rooted philosophical and legal tradition to work from. There is nothing such here. To the contrary, one of the most powerful of American myths up to the time of Wilson was that national traits disappeared on arrival at Ellis Island or its forebears. It may be averred that we had little choice *but* to embrace this reassuring expectation. Even so, we did so, and with a very considerable degree of success.[59]

There has even so been a contrarian tradition of outlandish, sometimes bizarre, ethnic hostility. Let us hear from Dr. Franklin, writing from Philadelphia, the City of Brotherly Love, in the year of Our Lord 1751. Newcomers were beginning to arrive from Germany (to this day known as the Pennsylvania Dutch). Which led Dr. Franklin to this sage observation:

[T]he Number of purely white People in the World is proportionably very small. All *Africa* is black or tawny. *Asia* chiefly tawny. *America* (exclusive of the new Comers) wholly so. And in *Europe*, the *Spaniards, Italians, French, Russians* and *Swedes*, are generally of what we call a swarthy Complexion; as are the *Germans* also, the *Saxons* only excepted, who with the *English*, make the principal Body of White People on the Face of the Earth. I could wish their Numbers were increased. And while we are, as I may call it, *Scouring* our Planet, by clearing *America* of Woods, and so making this Side of our Globe reflect a brighter Light to the Eyes of Inhabitants in *Mars* or *Venus*, why should we in the Sight of Superior Beings, darken its People? [W]hy increase the Sons of *Africa*, by Planting them in *America*, where we have so fair an Opportunity, by excluding all Blacks and Tawneys, of increasing the lovely White and Red? But perhaps I am partial to the Complexion of my Country, for such Kind of Partiality is natural to Mankind.[60]

In this spirit observe the evolution, or rather regression, of the ethnic stereotype of the American Irish in political cartoons in the second half of the nineteenth century, as recorded by Dale T. Knobel in his notable work, *Paddy and the Republic: Ethnicity and Nationality in Antebellum America.*[61] Beginning with a rough and primitive figure even so capable of becoming civilized, Paddy turns first into an object of ridicule, then later a subhuman, simian species born to inferiority and incapable of being a true American.[62] This pretty episode is very probably the first instance of Darwinian racism, if that is an acceptable term. Paddy regresses over time into an ape-like creature. As does blowsy, boozy Bridget. A two-panel British woodcut of the famine era shows first the Irish in Ireland as desperately distressed, but fully human; next, having migrated they become model Victorians in the new world. A generation later, Thomas Nast would depict them as brutes incapable of human sensibility. Interestingly, cartoons of the time in New York tended to contrast the simian Celt with blacks represented as respectable citizens with features that Phiz might have used in an illustration from Dickens.

One of the problems here is that the men who devised the doctrine of self-determination came to the subject as unlettered as ever Paddy arrived at a polling booth. Literally, they knew almost nothing of the subject. Wilson was open about this; disarmingly so. In the last draining hours of his doomed campaign for the treaty and the Covenant of the League, crossing the country and giving speeches from the rear of his train, he had this to say of Azerbaijan: "Do you know where Azerbaijan is? Well, one day there came in a very dignified and interesting group of gentlemen from Azerbaijan. I did not have time until they were gone to find out where they came from, but I did find this out im-mediately—that I was talking to men who talked the same language that I did in respect of ideas, in respect of conceptions of liberty, in respect of conceptions of right and justice."[63]

Wilson at his worst. He knew nothing of Azerbaijan; nothing of Azeris. A diplomacy based on the principle of self-determination entered what was literally largely unmapped territory. Just four years earlier, Walter Lippmann, who would accompany Wilson to Paris, laid out the difficulties in a brisk introduction to *The Stakes of Diplomacy:*

These difficulties are made more acute by the fact that the things we have to think about are so unreal to us. We are feeding on maps, talking of populations as if they were abstract lumps, and turning our minds to a scale unheard of in history. To how many of us does the word Slovak convey the picture of fathers and mothers and children, of human beings with habits and personalities as intimate as our own? Even to highly cultivated people the word Slovak probably calls up the association of "light pink patches with diagonal shading" somewhere in bewildering Austria-Hungary. How many people have ever heard of the Szekels of Transylvania? Yet there are over 800,000 of them, all entitled to a place in the sun and all capable of making trouble if it is denied to them. When you consider what a mystery the East Side of New York is to the West Side, the business of arranging the world to the satisfaction of the people in it may be seen in something like its true proportions.[64]

And yet, the President was no worse in this sense than the contemporaries with whom he would set about revising the rules of international society to accommodate, indeed to legitimize and even hallow the principle of ethnicity. At times his innocence verges on the credulous. Colonel House's diary has this entry of February 28, 1918:

last night at dinner, the President, Mrs. Wilson and I were discussing how ubiquitous Jews were; one stumbled over them at every move and they were so persistent that it was impossible to avoid them. I thought it surprising in view of the fact that there were so few in the world. This brought on an argument as to how many there were. I thought not more than fifteen million—twenty millions at the outside. Mrs. Wilson guessed fifty millions and the President one hundred millions. To settle it he sent the butler for a World's Almanac and was greatly surprised to find that in Europe there were less than ten millions, in Asia about a half million and in this country about three millions. He could not believe it even after he saw the figures. The reason I happened to hit the mark was that I remembered having read somewhere that one tenth of the Jews of the world were living in New York City. While I knew this was not strictly true, I thought it somewhere near the truth.[65]

Thus, we observe the then-President of the United States estimating that the size of the world Jewish population was in fact equal to that of the United States, which passed the 100 million mark just a few years earlier.[66] By contrast, House, then Wilson's personal representative to the Allied governments, and later a member of the American Commission to Negotiate Peace, was surprisingly accurate. Fifteen million would be a good estimate of the world Jewish population at that time, albeit with some uncertainty as to the size of the

Sephardic segment. One-tenth of the world's Jewish population would have been living in New York City. But House was the exception; Wilson the rule. Which is to say, no one knew much at all about this subject.

Including the other peacemakers in Paris. Charles Seymour, who would become president of Yale, was chief of the Austro-Hungarian division of the American delegation in Paris. In a letter home of May 31, 1919, he records this celebrated scene:

> We went into the next room where the floor was clear and Wilson spread out a big map (made in our office) on the floor and got down on his hands and knees to show us what had been done; most of us were also on our hands and knees. I was in the front row and felt someone pushing me, and looked around angrily to find that it was Orlando [Italian Premier and leader of the Italian delegation to the Conference], on *his* hands and knees crawling like a bear toward the map. I gave way and he was soon in the front row. I wish that I could have had a picture of the most important men in the world on all fours over this map.[67]

Yaleman Seymour's impression was not far different from that of Oxonian Harold Nicolson, who was serving as a member of the British delegation. He wrote to his wife Vita Sackville-West of Wilson, Lloyd George, and Georges Clemenceau: "darling, it is appalling, those three ignorant and irresponsible men cutting Asia Minor to bits as if they were dividing a cake."[68] But then nobody knew. *What* boundaries? Commissions were sent out. What is your nationality? Why, we are people of hereabouts. Paul Kennedy records that the mobilization orders to the Austro-Hungarian military went out from Vienna in fifteen languages.[69] But it may be doubted that any university in Europe, much less any chancery, had a linguistic map of the region, albeit there would have been linguistic censuses.

Wilson would have been distressed to learn he was so far off on such matters of consequence. It wouldn't have bothered Franklin D. Roosevelt the least little bit. He was going to win a war and establish an international organization and he did both. Details? Good heavens. In 1942 he explained in a letter to Field Marshall Jan Smuts that they would sort out this self-determination business through a "plebescite technique" which would effectively shift the burden of "political reorganization" of controversial territories. His idea was that ultimate sovereignty would be decided "when a conclusive majority was obtained after, if necessary, the holding of 'succeeding plebiscites until one side or the other makes a decision by overwhelming vote.' "[70]

As for membership in the new organization, that was negotiable. As early as 1943 the Soviet Union began to ask for representation for individual Soviet republics on post-war panels, especially the War Crimes Commission, arguing that these republics were no less sovereign than members of the British Dominions and that their participation in the war made them morally entitled to participate. Initially, Soviet insistence extended to the Ukraine, Belarussia, Moldavia, Lithuania, Latvia, Estonia, and the "Karelo-Finnish" Republic. However, in early 1944, the Soviet government announced that under the newly adopted Soviet constitution, republics were autonomous in foreign affairs and, therefore, all sixteen Soviet republics should be entitled to representation in international institutions.

The delegates to the August-September, 1944, Dumbarton Oaks conference were unable to resolve this issue. It did not, however, become a public controversy at this time. According to Russell, this was the only issue of any substance which was *not* discussed in James Reston's celebrated articles in the *New York Times* reporting the texts under consideration.[71]

Hull was "amazed" when the Soviet claim was reported to him. The President thought it "absurd." He told Under Secretary Stettinius emphatically that the United States could under no conditions accept such a proposal and instructed him to explain to Gromyko that it would present untold complications, and that it would be just as logical for the United States to ask for admission of the forty-eight states. The extraordinary concern engendered by the Soviet position was reflected in Roosevelt's decision to keep the whole matter restricted to the knowledge of the fewest possible people, partly because of the feeling that if it became widely known it might, in Hull's words, "blow off the roof . . . . "[72]

When President Roosevelt met with members of the Committee on Foreign Relations in January, 1945, he stated that the United States would insist on forty-eight votes if Stalin insisted on sixteen.

At the Yalta conference in February, 1945, the major issues relating to the United Nations were Security Council voting and membership for the Soviet republics. The Soviets began by insisting that Permanent Members of the Security Council be able to veto *discussion* of an issue, as well as to veto Council action. They yielded on this point. At the same time, the Soviets offered to reduce their membership demand from all sixteen republics to

ON THE "SELF-DETERMINATION OF PEOPLES"

three—Belarussia, the Ukraine, and Lithuania—given their size, importance, and suffering during the war. Then Stalin agreed to drop Lithuania. (This would have been difficult for Roosevelt to accept in that the United States still recognized the pre-war government, a member of the League.) However, Roosevelt did agree to support membership in the General Assembly for the Ukraine and Belarussia, as well as the U.S.S.R., which was the final resolution. Although the Soviet compromise on Security Council voting was reported to the public, the Yalta compromise on Soviet republics was kept secret.

When the compromise was reported to the members of the U.S. delegation to the San Francisco conference, however, reaction was decidedly negative: "Leahy thought it would be received 'very badly.' Byrnes considered it 'very unwise,' and reminded Roosevelt of the effective isolationist arguments in 1920 against the League of Nations, on the ground that the British would have five votes, because of the dominions, while the United States would have only one."[73] Senator Vandenberg noted in his diary: "This will *raise hell* . . . . It looks like a bad business to me. The Delegates were rather stunned."[74] As a result, Roosevelt wrote to Stalin and Churchill requesting that the United States *also* be given three votes in the General Assembly. This was agreed to as well.

At the end of March, word of the proposed arrangement leaked to the press, creating something of a storm. In his 998th, and last, press conference on April 5, 1945, President Roosevelt was queried on the issue and gave a long response. He downplayed the decision, portraying it as a personal request by Stalin on behalf of these devasted republics which Roosevelt said he supported for "sentimental" reasons. He added:

A. [The issue] is not really of any great importance. [The General Assembly] is an investigatory body only. . . .

Q. They don't decide anything, do they?

A. No.[75]

CHAPTER 3

National Proletarian Internationalism

*I*N his fine study of *The Union Republics in Soviet Diplomacy*, Vernon V. Aspaturian of Pennsylvania State University records and analyzes the background of the flurry at San Francisco. On February 1, 1944, the Soviet Union had

dramatically amended its Constitution . . . to permit its sixteen constituent Republics to establish separate foreign offices, diplomatic services, defense commissariats and national troop formations. By empowering each republic with the constitutional authority to engage in diplomatic relations, conclude international agreements and organize national armies, the Amendments intended to confer upon the Republics the missing legal essentials of statehood and sovereignty.[1]

Six months later the Soviets asked to have all sixteen

republics represented at the Dumbarton Oaks Conference held in Washington, where the plans for the postwar world organization were to be drafted. Aspaturian
writes that "Western official reaction fluctuated from an
apprehensive sarcasm to near panic."[2] What fiendish
game was afoot? In truth not all that much. "From the
standpoint of Soviet legal doctrine," Aspaturian continues, the Republics had "from the very beginning and
without interruption . . . been paraded as sovereign
states."[3] The principle of self-determination required
nothing less.

And so we turn again to the O.E.D. Self-determination: "The action of a people in deciding its own form of
government; free determination of statehood, postulated
as a right."[4] The first citation, as earlier noted, is to the
1911 edition of the Encyclopaedia Britannica. Thence to
the declarations of the Quadruple Alliance of 1917. Next
Wilson, 1918. But in fact, in its contemporary sense, the
term *first* appears in the Proclamation on the Polish
Question, adopted by the London Conference of the
First International, the International Workingmen's Association in 1865. The issue was placed on the agenda by
Marx himself. The proclamation declared the need "to
annihilate the growing influence of Russia in Europe by
assuring to Poland the right of self-determination which
belongs to every nation and by giving to this country
once more a social and democratic foundation."[5] This, at
all events, is how it is cited by E. H. Carr and others.[6]

The point was clear and the irony considerable. Carr
notes that it was sympathy with Poland that led to the
founding of the First International. Nationalism and
internationalism equally present at the creation. (Indeed,
at this time Marx wrote: "Formerly, I thought the

separation of Ireland from England impossible. Now I think it inevitable.")[7] Connor points out the irony that "this most famous credo of nationalism should make its first appearance in a public document which was drafted by history's most famous internationalist."[8] Strategically, there was no choice. The masses were at the barricades: but not as proletarian internationalists: rather, as Polish patriots. (Or whatever national group was involved. Marx is said never to have forgiven the Czech regiment that was deployed to suppress the Viennese uprising of 1848. No kin of theirs.) Marx and Engels seemed to have contrived a pact with their own particular devil of this time. Communists would support nationalist movements but, in Connor's words, "Communists themselves must remain above nationalism, this immunity being their single defining characteristic."[9] As we shall see, the immune system broke down.

Robert Conquest notes that "[f]rom Lenin's point of view, as from Marx's, international proletarian interests were the central issue, and nationality a temporary distraction. . . . 'Nation' was a category marking the epoch of capitalism. . . . Socialism would overcome this and, eventually, 'merge' the nations."[10] The Marxist commitment to self-determination for all national groups had been reaffirmed by the Second International when it met in London in 1896.[11] But in 1912, Lenin decreed that "the interests of socialism are above the right of nations to self-determination."[12] He accordingly set Stalin to work on a tract on Marxism and the national and colonial question. Stalin would sort it out.

With the twentieth century, praise God, coming to an end, it will seem a trifle late and a bit much to pore over yet again the interminable and innumerable tracts of this hardy band of idealists and sociopaths and sociopathic idealists, who so affected the beginning of the century. And yet, there is still something to be learned. Which is that for all that it proclaimed a doctrine of internationalism, from the outset communist politics were the politics of ethnicity. That those involved were committed Marxists none need doubt. Nor yet did they question the proposition that industrialization would create a new class of workers, an industrial proletariat. Nor, finally, that capitalism would inexorably become international in form and function, thus creating in theory certain common interests, or at least common conditions, as between national proletariats, from which would evolve an international proletariat. But what the Bolsheviks encountered on the ground was intense nationalist passion, tearing apart the old empires, that of the Czars included. *Nationalism and land distribution were the real dynamics of revolution in 1917, and the Bolsheviks embraced both.* This *was the contradiction in Bolshevism.* The workers and peasants were first to be divided among separate nations, thereafter to join hands as Workers of the World. The peasants were to be given land, thereafter to be taken from them and given to the collective.

Self-determination was incorporated into the program of the Second Congress of the Russian Social Democratic Labour Party in 1903. In an article, "The National Question in our Program," which appeared that year in *Iskra*, Lenin wrote: "the Social-Democrats will always combat every attempt to influence national self-determination by violence or by any injustice from without."[13] They were obsessed with ethnicity, or as they termed it,

The National Question. Engels, as Marx, had a passing interest in Irish matters, and Marx had an eye on imperialism. In their hugely informative treatment, *Soviet Disunion: A History of the Nationalities Problem in the USSR*, Bohdan Nahaylo and Victor Swoboda note that in his 1864 inaugural address to the *First* International in London, Marx remarked upon "the shameless approval, demonstrative sympathy or idiotic indifference with which Europe's upper classes observed Russia's conquest of the Caucasian fastnesses and her murder of heroic Poland."[14] It was just this "Russia," seething with ethnic and religious and nationalist conflict that the Bolsheviks seized in the name of a theory of class conflict that proclaimed the nonexistence or false consciousness of the former.

George Kennan, perhaps the most renowned of American students of Russia has recently noted that "nationalism has developed into the greatest emotional-political force of the age. . . . It has triumphed most decisively, in particular, over the radical Marxism that loomed so large as an emotional-political force for a time in the early decades of this century."[15]

To say again, this is the contradiction of Leninist communism that would so distort the twentieth century. Two incompatible movements were sweeping Europe. On the one hand, a great stirring of ethnic or nationalist sentiment. Typically, intellectuals gave form and content to these movements. Simultaneously, there were movements among industrial workers to organize and gain recognition as legitimate participants in economic decision-making in their respective realms. Again, intellectuals typically gave form and content to *these* movements. The utility of combining the two forces was inescapable, especially among Continental Marxists who could see in nationalism a tactical, interim device with which to destabilize the then dominant multi-ethnic regimes of that period, notably the Hapsburg, Romanov, and Ottoman empires. The Second International invited one and all to become nationalists in order the sooner to become internationalists.

As noted, the Bolsheviks joined in this enterprise in 1903. But in the same year Lenin offered this surpassingly obscure formulation: "as the party of the proletariat, [the Social-Democratic Party] considers it to be its positive and principal task to advance the self-determination of the working class within each nationality rather than the self-determination of peoples and nationalities."[16] Aspaturian notes that "By the time the Bolsheviks seized power, a considerable body of Communist literature on national self-determination was already in existence."[17] Engels had observed that Russia "could only be mentioned as the detainer of an immense amount of stolen property, which would have to be disgorged on the day of reckoning."[18] As the Bolshevik day of reckoning approached, disgorgement loomed ever larger as a matter of day-to-day politics. Internationalism was all very well, but what about Ukrainian separatism then and there? In the *Theses on the National Question* of 1913, Lenin stated that the self-determination of nations was "*absolutely* essential" to the party program:

THESES ON THE NATIONAL QUESTION
1. The article of our programme (on the self-determination of nations) cannot be interpreted to mean anything but *political* self-determination, i.e., the right to secede and form a separate state.

2. This article in the Social-Democratic programme is *absolutely* essential to the Social-Democrats of Russia

a) for the sake of the basic principles of democracy in general;

b) also because there are, within the frontiers of Russia and, *what is more, in her frontier areas*, a number of nations with sharply distinctive economic, social and other conditions; furthermore, these nations (like all the nations of Russia except the Great Russians) are unbelievably oppressed by the tsarist monarchy;

c) lastly, also in view of the fact that throughout Eastern Europe (Austria and the Balkans) and in Asia—i.e., in countries bordering on Russia—the bourgeois-democratic reform of the state that has everywhere else in the world led, in varying degree, to the creation of independent national states or states with the closest, interrelated national composition, has either not been consummated or has only just begun;

d) at the present moment Russia is a country whose state system is more backward and reactionary than that of *any* of the contiguous countries, beginning—in the West—with Austria where the fundamentals of political liberty and a constitutional regime were consolidated in 1867, and where universal franchise has now been introduced, and ending—in the East—with republican China. In all their propaganda, therefore, the Social-Democrats of Russia must insist on the right of all nationalities to form separate states or to choose freely the state of which they wish to form part.[19]

Next, anticipating Roosevelt, Lenin decreed that Social-Democrats "demand the settlement of the question of such secession only on the basis of a universal, direct and equal vote of the population of the given territory by secret ballot."[20]

The Great War was soon upon them. The war which, in Jonathan's Yardley's words, "turned upside down the entire world in which it was fought, leaving almost nothing unchanged and absolutely nothing for the better."[21] So much has happened since, but it has not taken all that much time, really. I once visited Lenin's apartments in the Kremlin. Behind his desk, near the celebrated telephone switchboard, there stands, presumably as he left it, a small bookcase given over to English and French authors. No more than glancing I recognized three authors with whom I have spoken in my lifetime. Bertrand Russell, G. D. H. Cole, and one whose name just won't come back. The spell of Marxism became such, the insistence that an international proletarian movement was an irresistible force taking mankind to an inevitable next and final stage of history, that what was only an interval, two, three generations, seems somehow an epoch. The epoch in turn seems defined in the terms of the dialectic of scientific socialism and other such inaccessible self-evident truths. All of which obscures the reality of continuing ethnic, nationalist, religious conflict. Aspaturian writes:

Whereas for Wilson self-determination had an absolute character and was the ethical justification for the dismemberment of the polyglot German, Hapsburg and Ottoman Empires, for the Bolsheviks it was essentially a utilitarian device of only transitory and relative moral relevance, designed to bring about the decomposition of all multinational states and colonial empires, including the Russian, insofar as dissolutions promoted the advance of the Communist Revolution.[22]

Fair enough. And yet, might it not also be true that reality on the ground was not much different for that period—*not* all that distant—and the present. E. J. Hobsbawm observes that "the best minds in the international socialist movement—and it contained some extremely powerful intellects—applied themselves to this problem: Kautsky and Luxemburg, Otto Bauer and Lenin, to name but a few."[23] Among others he includes Stalin for *Marxism and the National and Colonial Question,* "not so much for its modest, but not negligible . . . intellectual merits, but rather for its subsequent political influence."[24] "Especially," he adds in a footnote, "in the dependent world."[25]

And this is the point. The spell of Marxism was nowhere greater than in the colonial and post-colonial world. It was just that, a spell. On yet another personal note, it happens that in my youth I knew Kerensky. Now Kerensky did not know me, but he would come on occasion to speak at our high school in East Harlem, in New York City. Hence, as an adult I was aware that there had been *two* Russian revolutions in 1917. Not one. But in, say, New Delhi in the 1970s you could have an *argument* over whether this were even possible. The Bolsheviks roaring the "Internationale" had stormed the Winter Palace, overthrown the Czar, and that was the end of the matter and the beginning of history.

The subtitle of Richard Pipes's *The Formation of the Soviet Union,* is *Communism and Nationalism, 1917–1923.* He sets the scene:

But by late 1912 it became necessary for the Bolsheviks to issue a more specific programmatic statement. All the other major parties in Russia had adopted definite programs for the solution of the minority question. In August of that year, even the Mensheviks who until then had been reticent, began to advocate national-cultural autonomy. Something had to be done. Lenin had moved in the summer to Cracow, and there had the opportunity to witness personally the extent to which the national question had interfered with the development of the socialist movement in the Austrian Empire and in the neighboring provinces of Russian Poland. With great zeal, he applied himself at once to the study of the pertinent literature, which until then he had known only second-hand, principally from the writings of Karl Kautsky. He now read Bauer's chief work and Kautsky's criticism of Bauer, and then several books dealing with the minorities in Russia, especially the Jews and the Ukrainians. He also compiled population statistics and economic data. Before long, he realized that the nationality problem played a much more important role in the life of Russia in general, and of socialism in particular, than he had until then supposed. The potential ally, whose utilization he had posited fifteen years earlier, was immediately available as a weapon against the established regime in Russia. An alliance with the nationality movement—on the conditions previously laid down—was a vital necessity, but such an alliance required a concrete national program with which to approach and to win the sympathy of the minorities.[26]

The Bolsheviks in power soon enough came up against the contradiction in their approach to self-determination. On October 26, 1917, the list of the Council of the People's Commissars was read out to the Congress of the Soviets. Writing in 1949, Isaac Deutscher made what for that time would have been the politically correct observation that "eleven were intellectuals and only four workers." The contemporary student of ethnicity, however, will ask a different question. To which the answer is that fourteen were Slavs. Or thirteen Slavs, one Jew. Plus one affirmative-action appointment, a Georgian: Joseph Vissarionovich Djugashvili-Stalin—"Chairman of the Commissariat for Nationalities."[27]

Next, on November 2, 1917, "The Declaration of the Rights of the Peoples of Russia" written by Lenin and Stalin, was proclaimed. These Rights included "the right of the peoples of Russia to free self-determination, even to the point of separating and forming independent states."[28] On December 18 the Soviet Government decreed the independence of Finland, in a document signed by Lenin and Stalin. Deutscher comments:

> This magnanimous act harmonized with the programme which Stalin had outlined in his treatise on *Marxism and the Nationalities* in 1913. In it he championed the right of the peoples oppressed by the Tsarist Empire to self-determination; and he interpreted that principle in the sense that every oppressed people should be free to break away from Russia and constitute itself an independent state. It was true that socialism did not favour national separatisms and the formation of numberless small states all lacking viability. Its ultimate objective was international Socialist society. Real social and economic progress demanded, in the Socialists' view, the abolition of the barriers that kept nations apart. But international Socialist society could be founded, so Stalin had argued, only by voluntary agreement of the peoples that would form it; and voluntary agreement implied that each nation should first regain its complete freedom. Lenin defended this view in a witty comparison between that freedom and the freedom of divorce which was advocated by Socialists. "We hardly mean", said Lenin, "to urge women to divorce their husbands, though we want them to be free to do so." Similarly, the Bolsheviks pleaded for the right of the non-Russian peoples to secede from Russia, without encouraging separatist aspirations. . . .

The Bolshevik leaders hoped that the non-Russian nationalities would follow the Russian example and carry out their own revolutions; and that having obtained the right to divorce they would after all rejoin Russia in a free union of Socialist nations.[29]

Well, of course, they didn't. (Did and didn't. Immigrant Finnish lumbermen were at the forefront of the American socialist movement.

The pathbreakers were the Finnish Socialists. They were a relatively recent immigrant group: the peak of Finnish immigration was in the years 1899–1904. The leading authority on American Finnish Socialism [John Kolehmainen] writes: "Immigrant socialism was for many years a child of the old country. . . . As the new gospel's first apostle testified, 'Socialism is with us a kind of immigrant baggage.' " As with other ethnic groups, Socialism was part of a whole complex break with old traditions. The first Finnish Socialists preached atheism and science as well as Socialism, and their membership strength derived from anti-clericalism as well as from any specific grievances as workingmen.[30]

The present head of the American Communist Party, Mr. Gus Hall, was born Arvo Kusta Halberg. A great proportion of American Communists were ethnically "Russian.")

But again, the student of ethnicity will note the usage in the 1917 declaration: "the right of the peoples of Russia." How's that? Had the Georgians become one of the *Russian* peoples? Not Georgians in a Russian empire? Again, contradiction. Stalin was not oblivious to the "problem." As early as 1913 he was asking: "What is to be done with the Mingrelians, the Abkhasians, the Adjarians, the Svanetians, the Lesghians . . . . "[31] Or such exotica as "Caucasian Highland Jews" noted in "Marxism and the National Question."[32] It appears that Lenin had got him, in turn, to study the Austrians, such as Bauer, who were trying to work out the contradiction. Stalin showed himself skeptical.

And it is by no means fortuitous that the national programme of the Austrian Social-Democrats enjoins a concern for the "*preservation* and *development* of the national peculiarities of the peoples." Just think: to "preserve" such "national peculiarities" of the Transcaucasian Tatars as self-flagellation at the festival of *Shakhsei-Vakhsei*; or to "develop" such "national peculiarities" of the Georgians as the vendetta![33]

Shakhsei-Vakhsei refers to a ritual atonement of Shi'ite Muslims commemorating the death of Husain at Karbalah. How much he actually knew of this "peculiarity" is a matter of conjecture. As for the Georgian vendetta, however, Stalin raised this local custom to the level of an international institution.

In January 1918, with the Czarist empire breaking up all around them, Stalin told the third All-Russian Congress that as regards the equal rights of self-determination of peoples, some peoples were more equal than others. As described by Deutscher, Stalin argued that the principle "ought to be understood as the right of self-determination not of the *bourgeoisie* but of the toiling masses of a given nation. The principle of self-determination ought to be used as a means in the struggle for socialism and it ought to be subordinated to the principles of socialism."[34] Thus, the notion of nationalism as a bourgeois interest is a more prominent theme for Stalin. This work is not to be dismissed. He anticipates Horowitz in setting forth the exploitive measures which lead to attacks by the more backward group against the more advanced:

> But matters are usually not confined to the market. The semi-feudal, semi-bourgeois bureaucracy of the dominant nation intervenes in the struggle with its own methods of "arresting and preventing." The bourgeoisie of the dominant nation, whether large or small, is able to deal more "rapidly" and "decisively" with its competitors. "Forces" are united and a series of restrictive measures is put into operation against the "alien" bourgeoisie, measures passing into acts of repression. The struggle passes from the economic sphere to the political sphere. Limitation of freedom of movement, repression of language, limitation of franchise, restriction of schools, religious limitations, and so on are piled on to the head of the "competitor." Of course, such measures are designed not only in the interest of the bourgeois classes of the dominant nation, but also in pursuit of the specifically caste aims, so to speak, of the ruling bureaucracy. But from the point of view of the results achieved this is quite immaterial: the bourgeois classes and the bureaucracy in this matter go hand in hand—whether it be in Austria-Hungary or in Russia.[35]

George Will has recorded that Deutscher once told an Oxford audience that "proof of Trotsky's farsightedness" was that even then, years after his death, none of his forecasts had yet come true.[36] So, alas, with Stalin's expectations. He could handle Trotsky by murdering him, but murdering "peoples of Russia" by the millions could not overcome the contradiction in the Bolshevik concept of self-determination. Seven decades later the breakup of the Romanov empire resumed. In 1991, Aleksandr Solzhenitsyn described an "all-pervading ethnic bitterness": "From the vantage point of today, the more peaceful resolution, and the one holding much greater promise for the future, calls for a decisive parting of the ways for those who should separate. This is precisely due to the all-pervading ethnic bitterness that has obscured the rest of life: all else seems unimportant in the grip of a passion to which few of our people are immune."[37] He then offered a thought to which we will return. The thought that things weren't all that bad in the old regime:

The smallest national groups: the Nenets, Permyak, Evenki, Mansi, Khakas, Chukchi, Koryak, and other peoples I cannot enumerate here. They all lived well in the Tsarist "prison of peoples" and it is we, the communist Soviet Union, who have dragged them toward extinction. There is no calculating the wrongs they have suffered from our infamous administration and from our mindless and rapacious industry, which has brought pollution and ruin into their lands, destroying support systems especially vital for the survival of critically small groups. We must lose no time in offering our help in restoring them to life and vigor. It is not yet too late.

Every people, even the very smallest, represents a unique facet of God's design. As Vladimir Solovyov has written, paraphrasing the Christian commandment: "You must love all other people as you love your own."[38]

But . . . when it comes to living arrangements, you live with your own.

Solzhenitsyn's vision was the return of an entity that might be called "Rus." The Great Russians, Little Russians (Ukrainians), and White Russians, (Belarussians). The Russian heartland. ("We all sprang from precious Kiev.")[39] The remaining twelve republics and assorted jurisdictions must go. "*We don't have the strength* for the peripheries either economically or morally. *We don't have the strength*...."[40]

And so, there it is. The heart rejecting the body. And, of course, now even the heartland isn't going to stay together. In October 1991, the Senate Committee on Foreign Relations met over coffee with Pyotr K. Kravchanka, Minister of Foreign Affairs of the Republic of Belarus. He talked with conviction and calm of his country. With its great city of Minsk and, as he had just told the General Assembly, *its* culture: "F. Dostoevsky, composers I. Stravinsky and [D]. Shostakovich, artist M. Chagall, poet Apollinaire...."[41] It was clear by now that Great Russia will have to go it alone. Solzhenitsyn seems to understand this and to accept it.

A week later the Foreign Relations Committee gave a luncheon for Askar Akayev, the new President of the Republic of Kyrgyzstan who has resolved the Bolshevik contradiction by returning to the doctrine of self-determination *and* the American Declaration of Independence. He came with a formal statement.

Gentlemen!

In the Declaration of Independence of the USA in 1776, it was stated: "When in the Course of human events, it becomes necessary for one people to dissolve the political bands which have connected them with another, and to assume among the powers of the earth, the separate and equal station to which the Laws of Nature and of Nature's God entitle them, a decent respect to the opinions of mankind requires that they should declare the causes which impel them to the separation."

I consider it to be my duty, being guided by these very principles, to explain to you the causes impelling us to strive toward a severance of the rigid bands with the former Union of Soviet Socialist Republics.

—This Union never was a union in the true sense of the word. It was a unitary State with an imperial Center always operating on behalf of its imperial objectives, in many cases running counter to the interests of the Republics, or in any event—not taking these interests into account.

—This Center was always based upon force and force alone, on the military-industrial complex, on the organs of State Security, and the Army. When these foundations crumbled, the Center began to collapse catastrophically quickly. It is not possible to resuscitate it, in fact, this would even contradict the sacred principles of freedom and democracy. I understand, gentlemen, that the world community needs guarantees connected with the enormous military machine of the former Soviet Union, with the stockpiles of thermonuclear weapons which it has accumulated. Such guarantees, without a doubt, should be provided by the Economic Community Treaty signed by eight Republics, including ours on 18 October 1991, as well as the Treaty on a Military Defensive Alliance and the Treaty on Humanitarian Cooperation, which, according to the convictions of the Republic of [Kyrgyzstan], we should conclude.[42]

As for future association, the new President's references were to the European Community and N.A.T.O. As for authorities: Adam Smith, Jefferson, Madison, Hamilton.

But for the moment, the "all-pervading ethnic bitterness" combined with hollowness, disbelief, grasping for conviction of any kind. On November 7, 1991, back in St. Petersburg, newly rechristened, the Revolution Day parade was cancelled. Two Russian officers stood outside the Winter Palace bearing a portrait of Czar Nicholas. The *Washington Post* reported:

History came almost full circle today in this magical city of czars and revolutionaries, poets and bureaucrats, 74 years after the Bolsheviks seized power in November 1917.

For the past seven decades, the Communists have celebrated their revolution by staging a grandiose military parade outside the Winter Palace, the last stronghold of the provisional government that ruled Russia for eight months after the overthrow of the czar. The city's Communist elite would gather on a podium in Palace Square as hundreds of thousands of workers streamed past waving Soviet flags and carrying red banners proclaiming the inevitable victory of socialism over imperialism.

Today, the square was taken over by a bewildering variety of anti-Communist groups, from monarchists to anarchists to Hare Krishnas, hailing the collapse of the world's first socialist state while disagreeing on practically everything else. The participants in a day of festivities, which commemorated the rebirth of the former Russian capital as St. Petersburg after 70 years as Leningrad, included the pretender to the Russian throne, Grand Duke Vladimir Kirillovich, who had flown in from Paris.[43]

The parade in Moscow was also cancelled. The U.S.S.R. would not live out the year.

People—as Michael Polanyi, sometime professor of philosophy at Oxford University, would say—change their minds. Most people. The spell of Marxism, however, persisted to the moment of utter falsification and will no doubt continue on, impervious to experience. Again Hobsbawm:

Social revolutionaries have been keenly aware of the force of nationalism, as well as ideologically committed to national autonomy, even when it is not actually wanted, as among the

Lusatian Slavs, whose language is slowly retreating, in spite of the admirable efforts of the German Democratic Republic to foster it. The *only* form of constitutional arrangements which socialist states have taken seriously since 1917, are formulas for national federation and autonomy. While other constitutional texts, where they existed at all, have for long periods been purely notional, national autonomy has never ceased to have a certain operational reality. However, inasmuch as such regimes do not, at least in theory, identify with any of their constituent nationalities and regard the interests of each of them as secondary to a higher common purpose, they are non-national.

Hence . . . it was the great achievement of the communist regimes in multinational countries to limit the disastrous effects of nationalism within them.[44]

It is not reasonable to ask that had the subject of ethnicity been more intensively taught, or indeed, taught at all, in universities over the past half century or so, we would be spared such passages? Hobsbawm's entire work seems directed at explaining away, or even denying, what Connor has called the plain fact that "the vertical category of nationalism has proven far more powerful than the horizontal category of class consciousness."[45]

CHAPTER 4

Before the Fall

*H*AVING remarked how near at hand the events which shaped the twentieth century really are, it is curious how remote the immediately preceding age has become. It seems clear enough that Great Britain entered the First World War with no particular designs on the Ottoman Empire.[1] By 1915, however, a kind of imperialist imperative imposed itself. Crazy Lord Kitchener and Company got engaged in a new Great Game of establishing a vast new Afro-Asian British dominion, to be governed either from Simla in the East or, preferably, Khartoum in the West. That the Czar would finally have The Porte seemed clear enough. By 1916 things still were not going well and the French had to be brought in on the deal, as provided by the Sykes-Picot agreement.[2] But by 1917 this whole way of life was beginning to look antique. In the spring of 1917, to cite David Fromkin,

Sir Mark Sykes, who had worked out the terms of the administrative arrangements with the French, persisted in believing that the Sykes-Picot Agreement met current needs. In the spring of 1917 he wrote to Percy Cox, chief political officer of the British administration in Mesopotamia, that one of its virtues was that it was framed in such a way as not to violate the principles that Woodrow Wilson's America and the new socialist Russia espoused with respect to national self-determination and nonannexation. "The idea of Arab nationalism may be absurd," he wrote, "but our Congress case will be good if we can say we are helping to develop a race on nationalist lines under our protection."[3]

"[H]elping to develop a race on nationlist lines under our protection." Jews had to be provided for, of course, lest a German-Jewish entente survive the Hohenzollerns. This was doable. "T. E. Lawrence told the Eastern Committee [of the Cabinet] that 'there would be no difficulty in reconciling Zionists and Arabs in Palestine and Syria, provided that the administration of Palestine remained in British hands.' "[4] The French started being difficult, a mode of negotiation that persists to this day.

On 5 October 1918 Leo Amery noted in his diary: "Talk with Sykes about what to do with the Sykes-Picot Agreement. He has evolved a new and most ingenious scheme by which the French are to clear out of the whole Arab region except the Lebanon" and in return get all of Kurdistan and Armenia "from Adana to Persia and the Caucasus." But the French did not agree.[5]

The rest, as they say, is history.

The British proceeded to set up a government in Iraq "on nationalist lines." Of which there were none. An American missionary cautioned Gertrude Bell, that most idealistic of camp followers, now assistant to the civil administrator: "You are flying in the face of four millenniums of history if you try to draw a line around Iraq and call it a political entity! Assyria always looked to the west and east and north, and Babylonia to the south. They have never been an independent unit. You've got to take time to get them integrated, it must be done gradually. They have no conception of nationhood yet."[6] There were half a million Kurds who would never accept Arab rule. Two million Shi'ites would not accept Sunni rule. (A Holy War was soon proclaimed against Britain in Karbalah.)

Elie Kedourie gave over a life of scholarship to the ironic proposition, as Martin Peretz wrote in the *New Republic*, that "the great revenge of imperialism was nationalism itself." He was born in Baghdad at a time when Jews were the plurality in that city, and quite the most considerable people in the region, with commercial contacts ranging from Manchester to Bombay to Shanghai. "[H]e watched—first up close, then from London—some of the most hateful ideologies of our time take root and prosper."[7] When George Kennan devotes a chapter in a recent work to "The Nation" it is Kedourie whom he quotes to set the tone.[8] Kedourie's defining essay, "'Minorities,'" included in his collection *The Chatham House Version and Other Middle-Eastern Studies*, describes the near permanent ethnic terror that settled onto Mesopotamia once "independence" came to Iraq. He records "the moving protest . . . of a young British officer, straight and upstanding and true, one of those whom the genius of England knew so well how to nurture and rear."[9] James Saumarez Mann by name, who found himself a district officer, in the old colonial usage, in the Middle Euphrates in 1918. He would be killed in 1920. In the meantime, he wrote to a British publication:

The problem is, of course, how to provide a native government with the force required to govern a wild and very mixed race divided by the bitterest religious hostilities and tribal feuds, and containing in its midst also colonies of fiercely hated Jews and Christians. . . .

We are dealing with people who have lost all consciousness of nationality in the political sense, who have from time immemorial been governed by foreigners, and among whom indeed the very word "Arab" is used scornfully.[10]

The Jews of Baghdad, familiar with conquest, having been in and about Babylon for some while, petitioned for British citizenship. They were turned down. Kedourie writes that a "bare thirty years sufficed to destroy their community and achieve their ruin." The Christian Assyrians fared no better. Their patriarch would petition for a measure of self-government under his direction, from precedent: "The temporal power has not been assumed by me, but it has descended to me from centuries past as a legalised delegation of the people to the patriarch. It was not only tolerated, but also officially recognised in the past by the old Sasanid kings, Islamic caliphs, Moghul khans and Ottoman sultans."[11] In good time the exile began. Kedourie relates:

[T]he unvocal masses and the colonies of Jews and Christians in their midst were handed over . . . to a band of men who were, to start with, for the most part, minor bureaucrats or little officers in the Ottoman service, and who were moved with certain crude and virulent notions, spreading from

Europe and picked up second-hand in Constantinople, Cairo and the ports of the Levant; men narrow and ignorant, devoid of loyalty and piety, of violent and ungovernable impulses.[12]

Some of these events were influenced by personality:

the genial eccentricity of Mr. Philby, proposing to make a thug who took his fancy the president of an Iraqi republic; . . . the fond foolishness of Miss Bell, thinking to stand godmother to a new Abbassid empire; . . . the disoriented fanaticism of Colonel Lawrence, proclaiming that he would be dishonoured if the progeny of the sharif of Mecca was not forthwith provided with thrones.[13]

Details: The new regime was installed to rule Iraq in 1921. Seventy years later the British were back, this time under the auspices of the United Nations as distinct from the earlier League of Nations. The Sunni Iraqis were still at war with the Kurds, still slaughtering Shi'ites in and about Karbalah. But to reach the Jews of Baghdad they had to aim missiles at Jerusalem and Tel Aviv. The Assyrians, however, were harder to reach. Most of them now lived in Chicago. Starting in 1933, they had simply fled Iraq.

The patriarch of the Assyrians had spoken the essential truth. Not a simple truth, but a reasonably consistent one. His congregation, better known as Nestorian, descended from Nestorius, a Syrian by origin, who became patriarch of Constantinople in 428 and taught the dual nature, divine and human, of Christ. Ecclesiastical discord had followed century on century, but accompanied by an impressive display of tolerance or even protection from kings, caliphs, khans, sultans. The Nestorians moved their capital to Baghdad at the outset of the five-hundred-year era of the Abbasid caliphs there. *The Encyclopedia of Religion* informs us: "the Nestorians were the first to promote Greek science and philosophy by translating Greek texts into Syriac and then into Arabic. They were highly favored by the caliphs and were the first to introduce Greek medicine into Baghdad."[14] They made their way to China and to South India, and who knows what might have come to pass had the Mongols not appeared. (Solzhenitsyn writes of "the terrible calamity of the Mongol invasion" visited upon the Rus.[15] Mind, Mongols have not of late had much to say in either matter. Now they are a minority within the Han Chinese empire and beginning to assert themselves in that role. A recent *New York Times* dispatch records that "more and more Mongols [in the P.R.C.] are asserting their ethnic heritage," having created the General Coordination Committee of Inner Mongolian Rejuvenation Movements.)[16] Still, Genghis Khan could not or did not drive them from Mesopotamia. Self-determination did that. Much as even then it was driving Greeks from Anatolia, the English from Ireland, Magyars from Rumania, and so across the map of the war-torn world.

Rumania. In 1947 Solomon F. Bloom, professor of history at Brooklyn College, and author of *The World of Nations: A Study of the National Implications in the Work of Karl Marx* (1941), published in *Commentary* an almost lyrical account of his childhood and youth in Harlau, a small market town in the northern corner of old Rumania. The author's note sums up the matter nicely: "This autobiographical footnote to history brightly illuminates the process by which the principle of national self-determination, after World War I, tore apart the fabric of harmonious living among the varied peoples of the old Austrian and Turkish Empires and left them the embattled racists of today."[17] The Jews of Harlau were a class-ridden lot. "The snobbism of the poorest merchant and his family toward the richest of master craftsmen was intense, unbending, and fully repaid in resentment."[18] But if anyone else was aware of this, or being aware bothered to care, Bloom seems not to have noticed, and there does not seem to be much he *didn't* notice.

There were several nationalities in town, in addition to the Jews. A few expatriated Austrian subjects practiced their hereditary craft of pottery . . . . I do not remember their linguistic affiliation, but I think they were Slovaks . . . . A Russian group, called *Lipovani*, had settled in town mainly as hog-raisers and butchers for the peasant trade.

Then there were Germans. Two families of German wheelwrights turned out the better carriages and wheels for Harlau . . . . The pharmacist was a German from Austria, who regarded Rumanians and Jews with impartial contempt. You wiped your feet in the summer, or your boots in the winter, before intruding into his sparklingly clean and confusingly scented Holy of Holies . . . .

A few Levantines—Greeks, Armenians, Turks—were engaged in characteristic businesses such as cafes and candy stores. . . . One of the cafes, which served non-alcoholic drinks, mostly tea and coffee, was operated by a native of Asia Minor whom our elders assigned to the people of the notorious Haman. Our *timkhe*—Hebrew for "miserable"—was a quiet and likable old fellow, but on Purim, when we celebrated the fall of the tyrant who proposed to exterminate the Jews, he shut up shop, drew the blinds, and went into a kind of mourning. Our Purim was his Yom Kippur.

The itinerant merchants were as mixed as the residents. Only the Turks sold coffee grinders, for instance. The traveling salesmen who peddled prayer-books and shawls and phylacteries generally came from Austria. A contractor from Italy built our new town hall . . . . He brought his own gang of skilled masons, who settled in town for a whole year, with their families, to complete the job. . . . Movement was still free in central Europe. We drank coffee, prayed, and built houses on lines stretching from Italy to Turkey to Austria.[19]

Bloom is frank to say that "neither the Jews nor the other groups got along so well with the native Rumanian population that surrounded and engulfed them."[20] But so long as the Rumanians held "the national monopoly of administrative, bureaucratic, and political offices; of the jobs, the nuisance value, and the graft," all was comparatively symbiotic and peaceful.[21]

Solzhenitsyn writes of a not dissimilar past.

In the course of three-quarters of a century, to the sound of incessant proclamations trumpeting "the socialist friendship of peoples," the communist regime has managed to neglect, entangle, and sully the relationship among these peoples to such a degree that one can no longer see the way back to the peaceful coexistence of nationalities, that almost drowsy nonperception of distinctions that had virtually been achieved— with some lamentable exceptions—in the final decades of pre-revolutionary Russia.[22]

Still stunned by events of the twentieth century, Europeans seem almost averse to the history of the preceding era. Make it *all* go away, is as much as many can manage. For Americans there is a different problem. We seem possessed by a positive need to believe that the

Europe of the Hapsburgs, Hohenzollerns, Romanovs was a setting of implacable tyranny imposed with singular viciousness upon minorities that Bloom and Solzhenitsyn tell us lived together in relative harmony, indeed synergy. The received American view is emphatically otherwise. Life was miserable there and the miserable fled here and were welcomed and God was well pleased with his servants. Thus Emma Lazarus in her good/bad poem "The New Colossus," affixed now to the pedestal of the Statue of Liberty in New York harbor:

> Give me your tired, your poor,
> Your huddled masses yearning to breathe free,
> The wretched refuse of your teeming shore,
> Send these, the homeless, tempest-tossed, to me:
> I lift my lamp beside the gold door.

The centenary of the Statue of Liberty in 1986 brought this to mind, and I contributed this comment to *New York* magazine.

Emma Lazarus: God love her. She was obviously a lovable person. The *Dictionary of American Biography* describes her as having been born in 1849 "in New York City of pure Sephardic stock, the daughter of Moses and Esther (Nathan) Lazarus. A member of a large, wealthy, and devoted family, she passed a pleasant youth, with winters in New York City and summers by the sea."

Lazarus's first volume of poetry attracted the attention of Emerson, who invited her to spend a week in Concord. She went on to fiction, a five-act poetic drama set in seventeenth-century Italy, articles for *Scribner's*, and all manner of pleasant and useful things, until it came to that sonnet on the Statue of Liberty. . . .

There has come down to us a national memory of three migrations. First, the Protestant English of New England. The standard of living, if you like, of these seventeenth-century folk was as near to subsistence as life allows, but they leave no memory of destitution. To the contrary, the higher faculties and finer things preoccupy them at all times. The Pilgrims, two months and five days outbound from Plymouth, pause before setting ashore, to draw up a charter guaranteeing manhood suffrage.

Next (or simultaneously, really) is the forced migration of Africans in the slave trade, with its pervasive aggression and horror. . . .

Then come the Irish, followed by the central and southern Europeans, mostly Catholic and Jewish. And oh, what a sorry bunch and what a sorrowful time *that* was.

Nonsense. The 20 million-odd immigrants who arrived between 1870 and 1910 were not the wretched refuse of anybody's shores. They were an extraordinary, enterprising, and self-sufficient folk who knew exactly what they were doing, and doing it quite on their own, thank you very much. Just as important, the Europe they left behind had attained a general degree of civility and legality unknown in its history. If political rights were not always advanced, civil rights generally were. In 1861, the Italians had pulled off the Risorgimento, a brilliant democratic coup with scarcely a drop of blood shed. The newcomers did not learn the rule of law in New York: More likely, they noticed a regression.

It is true that the "Famine Irish" of the 1840s were destitute and driven, but there was already an ample Irish presence in the United States. (The St. Patrick's Day parade in New York, dating from 1762, is the oldest public festivity in the United States.) The continental migration that followed was somewhat driven by economic forces, but in the main it was a straightforward response to economic opportunity.

As to oppression of ethnic groups, one might well ask about pogroms. To which I responded in the *New York* article:

A fair question—which I think however, makes the point. In *History of the Jews of Poland and Russia*, Simon N. Dubnow gives no exact numbers of Jewish deaths in the pogroms of the 1880s, but the impression is that they were not large. The *Encyclopaedia Judaica* records, "The last great outburst occurred in June 1884 in Nizhni Novgorod . . . where the mob attacked the Jews of the Kanavino quarter, killing nine of them and looting much property. The authorities tried over 70 of the rioters and severe penalties of imprisonment were imposed on them."

Again, not much murder by twentieth-century standards, yet quite enough to shock the civilized world of that time. Just so, the 1882 political murder of two officials in Phoenix Park in Dublin near to convulsed British political society.

Put plain, the immigrants of the second half of the nineteenth century came from societies more civilized than ours. So much so that we have almost forgot, and should remember, for I don't think this myth of misery and degradation helps at all. Some people like it, I know, but it doesn't help. In particular, it doesn't help explain the *strengthening* of American democracy in the age of immigration.

There *was* a huge wave of immigrants. I would expect it was, in considerable proportion, a response to the huge wave of agricultural exports that began to reach Europe once the railroads reached our Midwest. Stanley Lebergott reckons that a third of a million European farms "in a long arc from England and Denmark through Prussia on into Russia" were closed down by American competition. Wheat acreage in England dropped 40 percent from 1869 to 1887. "The small capitalist farmers of North America hacked away at the economic base of the ruling landed classes in Europe more destructively than all the revolutionaries on the Continent." The displaced peasantry arrived just in time to catch the industrial dynamic that commenced in the Civil War. Steel production in the United States went from 77,000 tons in 1870 to 28 million tons in 1910. All the work of these homeless, tired, tempest-tossed folks.[23]

The Europe they left behind remained tolerant, confident—over confident, of course, as we know, but livable in a fashion that ought not be lost to memory. Here is Bloom's peroration on his beloved Harlau.

Shall I mention the Gypsies? They were too vagrant, and belonged—or rather didn't belong—everywhere. Their long trains of covered wagons, brimming over with pots, rugs, and infants, would be rushed through town by the rural gendarmes. They were not allowed to settle in populated places; one came on their camps at the roadside. The Gypsies were reputed to steal little girls, presumably for the white slave trade, and mothers were alert whenever they were known to be in the neighborhood. . . . The more positive contribution of the Gypsies was metal-working, tinkering, fiddling, fortune-telling, and trading in horses—not always their own, it was whispered.

With all their Bohemian color, the Gypsies were merely a patch on the Joseph's coat which was the Harlau district. The countryside was varied, although less so than the town. Rather than just Rumanian, the district was Rumanian-German-Jewish-Bulgarian-Ruthenian-Greek, to be brief. Only politics was dully uniform and integral; all else was multiform, kaleidoscopic, characteristically Central European. The whole of the area lying between Western Europe and the farther reaches of Russia and the East was more than a frozen ethnological mosaic; it was a living organism functioning through ethnic divisions of labor. In "much of Central Europe"—I quote from C. A. Macartney's *Problems of the Danube Basin* (Cambridge, 1942, pp. 45–6)—the market gardeners are "Bulgarians; the stop-me-and-buy-one men, Macedonians; the horse copers, hangmen, and fiddlers, Gypsies; the itinerant besom-binders, Slovaks. Some villages of Albania, the Rhodopes and Hungary consist almost entirely of masons and bricklayers. The male population of one such village in southwest Hungary built much of the Turkish capital of Ankara, and no mean proportion of the new buildings in Park Lane [London]." Such "nations" are functional more than linguistic. "You are a subtle nation, you physicians," wrote Ben Jonson—in an age when the West, too, wore a variegated aspect.

High-school boys in Harlau, strolling self-importantly of an evening on Strada Stefan cel Mare, spoke French almost habitually; especially the older ones in addressing the younger! They had first exchanged Yiddish for Rumanian and then had spurned Rumanian. The educated classes all over Central Europe, whether in town or country, preferred French, and sometimes German, to their native tongues. But the new "national" state must promote and impose a distinctive language; and this language, on the notion of self-determination, must be the rudest and least developed—that of the benighted rural population. As the energetic and skillful classes were subjected to peasant leadership, and the town to the country, the advanced culture was subordinated to the barely literate. Can any country progress if its urban elements are shorn of influence? Has any country ever done so?

Society moved backward, but statesmen like Woodrow Wilson, who added their powerful voices to the demands for national self-determination, didn't know why. Wilson, for example, was brought up in two American states—Georgia and South Carolina—which had extraordinary homogeneity of ethnic origin and tradition. Wilson's contemporary, Thorstein Veblen, knew better; a century ago, when Veblen was born, his native Minnesota consisted of an ingrown group of recent Norwegian immigrants, a sharply set-off community of Irish Catholics, and a Yankee-dominated town population. The divisions, as in Harlau, were economic as well as religious and cultural. Now suppose Minnesota had become a "national" state whose favors and advantages were assigned exclusively to one of the three groups. . . . No wonder Veblen wrote, in 1917, that "full and free self-determination runs counter to the rule of live and let live."

Veblen was closer to Harlau than Wilson. I thought of him as I watched motion pictures taken in my home town in the mid-thirties. I could hardly believe my eyes. My memory painted it as a bright little community, with a busy main street, punctuated by smart store-signs. The latter-day reality was dismal and dilapidated.

In the features of Harlau, as in those of the rest of Central Europe, was written the terrible depression of the twenties. The empires of the Hapsburgs and Romanovs had been dismantled and with them the economic patterns they had embodied. National and tariff walls were proliferated and rose higher and higher, until life was confined in prison cells. Men made themselves smaller to enter them, like Milton's devils squeezing into Pandaemonium to listen to Satan:

> . . . they but now who seem'd
> In bigness to surpass Earth's Giant Sons
> Now less than smallest Dwarfs, in narrow room
> Throng numberless. . . .

Then came Hitler. The mosaic of traditional variety and cunning interplay of parts was broken up entirely. The pieces of glass flew apart. The great hammer came down. Harlau, with countless other towns and cities, was ground into dust.[24]

The same Hitler whose first great adventure took place in the name of self-determination. Whose last would be the near extermination of Gypsy and Jew alike.

Waugh was likewise critical of the notion that self-determination could be expected to bring contentment to the "peoples" of Bloom's hometown: "The Austro-Hungarian Empire fell because the component peoples were urged to attribute their ills to thwarted nationalism. No one, I suppose, in their former dominions had a happier or better life as the result of 'self-determination'. . . . "[25] Surely that was Bloom's conclusion.

As the summer of 1991 passed, Isaiah Berlin, at 82, reflected on the century, "the worst century that Europe has ever had. . . . Worse, I suspect, even than the days of the Huns."[26] And why? Because "In our modern age, nationalism is not resurgent; it never died. Neither did racism. They are the most powerful movements in the world today, cutting across many social systems."[27] He ended "I am glad to be as old as I am."[28]

CHAPTER 5

Order in an Age
of Chaos

*I*N a remarkable address to a Joint Meeting
of the United States Congress in June of 1992, Boris N.
Yeltsin told of the new order in his ancient land. All had
changed from that which preceded, but of all such
things, one thing most: "We are firmly resolved not to lie
anymore."[1] *The Economist* had already noticed. Marxism-
Leninism was gone. It had "succeeded in poisoning half
the world's political life" for most of the century.[2] It had
"misled" so many "of the young governments of the
newly independent . . . third world" following the
Second World War.[3] Good-bye to all that. But now. *Now*
what story will we tell ourselves?

Which is to say, what is to be the basis of a legitimate
political order? The will of the people? Well, yes. But
which people? The cold war kept that question at bay.

No longer. Thus C. P. Cavafy, writing years ago of things to come.

> What are we waiting for, assembled in the public square?
>
> The barbarians are to arrive today.
>
> Why such inaction in the Senate?
> Why do the Senators sit and pass no laws?
>
> Because the barbarians are to arrive today.
> What further laws can the Senators pass?
> When the barbarians come they will make the laws.

But then.

> Why this sudden unrest and confusion?
> (How solemn their faces have become.)
> Why are the streets and squares clearing quickly,
> and all return to their homes, so deep in thought?
>
> Because night is here but the barbarians have not come.
> Some people arrived from the frontiers,
> and they said that there are no longer any barbarians.
>
> And now what shall become of us without any barbarians?
> Those people were a kind of solution.[4]

A year of our thought experiment went by. The barbarians had gone; barbarism had returned. Europe, a not insignificant portion of it, had become the setting of sealed trains, "ethnic cleansing," murderous hate. The *New York Times* warned that "The blood from the Balkans is seeping under Europe's door."[5] In what had been Yugoslavia a Serb militiaman, part of a force besieging the Bosnian city of Gorazde, told of his village burnt, his brother-in-law dead, "Serbs, naked and tortured." He had responded in kind. "I have cut the throats of three Turks so far, and I don't ever have nightmares".[6] Nor the rest of the world. More a matter of solemn faces, vague unrest. Let us end our thought experiment with *The Economist* of August 8, 1992, one year having passed. The Yugoslav headline states simply: "A war that gets harder to watch." The article recounts the continuing carnage: "Snipers kill refugee babies and at their funeral mortar bombs rain upon the mourners. Reports spread of killing and torture at Serbian detention camps. Around Sarajevo airport the fighting gets so bad that the United Nations has to stop flights with food and medicine for the starving city."[7]

Mind, the United States Senate passed a law of sorts, a Resolution calling for the use of force under Article 42 of the Charter. Citing in particular the provision for "demonstrations, blockade, and other operations by air, sea, or land forces . . . . " This act was not passive, and should have consequences. As a new era begins there is at least the possibility that a now more confident world order, working from a reasonable commitment to international law, a realistic deployment of international organization, might provide an alternative to—well— pandaemonium. But first the West, generally speaking, must get past the confusion that followed the sudden end of the cold war. Fukuyama writes of "This strange, sudden quiescence in the foreign policy debate."[8] The source of this quiescence is surely evident; he goes on to cite Kissinger's warning, whilst still Secretary of State in the 1970s, that "for the first time in our history we face the stark reality that the [Communist] challenge is unending."[9] This reflected the "realist position" in foreign policy. But realism proved altogether out of touch with reality! In a fine essay in the *American Scholar*, "Why Were We Surprised?", W. R. Connor suggested that realism was the *problem*, that we confined our analysis of the Soviet Union to "hard," quantifiable (or so we thought) measures that made no provision for "the passions—the appeal of ethnic loyalty and nationalism, the demands for freedom of religious practice and cultural expression, and the feeling that the regime had simply lost its moral legitimacy."[10] The student of ethnicity will have no difficulty recognizing these categories. Nor is there anything necessarily sentimental in speaking of passions. To the contrary; that *is* realism. In twentieth-century American political thought, none has understood this so well as Reinhold Niebuhr. In a sermon, "Law, Conscience, and Grace," given on the first Sunday of Lent, 1961, he expanded on this passage from St. Paul's Epistle to the Romans: "There will be tribulation and distress for every human being who does evil, the Jew first and also the Greek."[11] Niebuhr commented: "Collective egotism, particularly the collective arrogance of the races, is tremendous."[12] The races; of which Cavafy sung: Jew and Greek, Mede, Roman, Syrian, Cappadocian, Armenian, Parthian, Egyptian . . . all. Cavafy, the Alexandrian Greek, wrote often of fallen states, conquered peoples, and of stoic memories that followed. Images, allegories, yet reality also. In an introduction to *The Complete Poems* written also in 1961, W. H. Auden repeats Niebuhr's warning almost to the word: "In most poetic expressions of patriotism, it is impossible to distinguish what is one of the greatest human virtues from the worst human vice, collective egoism."[13]

"Realism" ignores such categories at the risk of irrelevance. Indeed, in the great game of semantic infiltration, to employ Fred Ikle's marvelous term, there has been no greater success than that of the nineteenth-century romantics who, in the foreign policy debates of twentieth-century America, got their adversaries to call them realists. On the other hand, Fukuyama presents us with the dilemma of the "neo-Wilsonians" who, in the light of the democratic revolutions that accompanied the end of the cold war, "believe that democracy and respect for human rights ought to be the central theme of U.S. policy."[14] Like it or no, Wilson defined twentieth-century American foreign policy in just such terms, and to a considerable degree democratic nations elsewhere have embraced this perspective. The question that will repeatedly occur, however, is the intensely practical question of sorting out such values in the context of ethnic group demands in which people define whom they love by whom they hate.

In practice this question repeatedly comes down to one of recognition by existing states of new states. At the turn of the century, James Crawford writes, "some fifty acknowledged States constituted the world community."[15] This number is now approaching two hundred. All of the new states having been carved out of preceding entities. This suggests that a fair amount would have been learned as to how the procedure works. But no, Crawford continues: "There is no generally accepted and satisfactory modern legal definition of statehood."[16]

Historically, both the comparatively simple issue of the recognition of governments and the question of recognition of states have caused enormous controversy.

Regarding recognition of states, scholars and foreign ministries have debated whether recognition has a constitutive effect or is merely declaratory of pre-existing fact. Hans Kelsen's classic 1941 article on recognition begins: "The problem of recognition of states and governments has neither in theory nor in practice been solved satisfactorily. Hardly any other question is more controversial . . . . "[17] The result, as one international law text allows, is that "Recognition is one of the most difficult topics in international law."[18]

But when the question arises as to whether an ethnic sub-unit within a state is entitled to self-determination and recognition, the legal complexity grows exponentially. From its first appearance, the legal community has demonstrated a clear hostility toward the concept of a *legal right* of "self-determination" which, Crawford notes, "would be a most significant exception to the traditional notion that the creation of states is a matter of fact and not law."[19] Existing states are, of course, the basic building blocks, the actors and subjects of international law. The attitude toward the proposition that there exists a legal right of self-determination in the early days of the League of Nations was best expressed in the report of the Rapporteurs appointed by the League to study the request by the Swedish-speaking inhabitants of the Aaland Islands to be allowed "self-determination." They desired to leave the newly independent Finnish state and to join Sweden. The issue was compounded by Sweden's anxiety over Finnish plans to fortify the islands which lie off Stockholm. The language of the islands is Swedish, as is indeed the language of a not insignificant minority in southern Finland. The report presented to the League by the Commission of Rapporteurs states plainly that the principle of self-determination

is not, properly speaking a rule of international law and the League of Nations has not entered it in its Covenant. This is also the opinion of the International Commission of Jurists. . . . It is a principle of justice and of liberty, expressed by a vague and general formula which has given rise to most varied interpretations and differences of opinion. . . . To concede to minorities, either of language or religion, or to any fractions of a population the right of withdrawing from the community to which they belong, because it is their wish or their good pleasure, would be to destroy order and stability within States and to inaugurate anarchy in international life; it would be to uphold a theory incompatible with the very idea of the State as a territorial and political unity. . . . The separation of a minority from the State of which it forms a part and its incorporation in another State can only be considered as an altogether exceptional solution, a last resort when the State lacks either the will or the power to enact and apply just and effective guarantees.[20]

And yet, thirty-four years later at San Francisco, this "altogether exceptional solution" was incorporated in the United Nations Charter as a "principle" of the international order. "[S]elf-determination of peoples." Nothing daunted, Crawford, in the tradition of commentary since Grotius and before, pronounces the Charter "cryptic."

There has been since 1945 perhaps no more divisive issue among writers . . . than the question whether there exists a legal right or principle of self-determination of peoples. Self-determination as a legal principle would represent a significant erosion of the principle of sovereignty. . . .

Thirty years later a vast literature and several advisory opinions of the International Court have failed to settle the matter.[21]

The majority of existing states, notably the previous "colonies," were willing enough to support the "self-determination" of Italian Somaliland and British Guyana, but surely not Biafra, Kurdistan, or a host of similar ethnic enclaves within the newly created states. If the references to "self-determination" in the Charter are "cryptic," there is nothing tentative about Article 2(7): "Nothing contained in the present Charter shall authorize the United Nations to intervene in matters which are essentially within the domestic jurisdiction of any state . . . . " "Self-determination" is a right, but "secession" and "civil war" are none of the world's business.

This defining fuzziness emerged from the 1960 General Assembly debate on Resolution 1514, a "Declaration on the Granting of Independence to Colonial Countries and Territories." (Since cited with approval by the International Court and the Security Council.) Appropriately enough, the proposal came from the Chairman of the Council of Ministers of the U.S.S.R., as the Yearbook of the United Nations has it, Nikita S. Khrushchev, who in his address to the General Assembly of September 23 of that year, declared the time had come for "the complete and final liberation of peoples languishing in colonial bondage." The Bolshevik tradition was alive and well. Soviet representatives went on to extol "the national liberation movements" of Asia and Africa. The United Kingdom asked for time, noting the Soviet engorgement of Eastern Europe, including the world's "three newest colonies"—Lithuania, Estonia, and Latvia. To no avail. Whereupon Cambodia, which would learn more of this matter, produced a draft sponsored by forty-three Asian and African states, which in the end was adopted by a vote of eighty-nine to none with nine abstentions.[22] No state could oppose the principle of self-determination. But note: self-determination *once.* The General Assembly simultaneously declared:

(2) All peoples have the right to self-determination. . . .

(4) All armed action of repressive measures of all kinds directed against dependent peoples shall cease in order to enable them to exercise peacefully and fully their right to complete independence . . . .

Then:

(6) Any attempt aimed at the partial or total disruption of the national unity and the territorial integrity of a country is incompatible with the purposes and principles of the Charter of the United Nations.[23]

In essence, it is illegal to aid secessionist or insurgent movements, but equally illegal to use force to prevent "self-determination."[24]

That secession itself is not considered illegal *per se* is evident from state practice, as the new representatives of Kazakhstan and Kyrgyzstan can attest. Even more striking, perhaps, the United Nations had long since admitted Pakistan in 1947 as a member when it split from British India, and then admitted Bangladesh as a member when it left Pakistan.[25] But withal, the rules of the game were established to favor *existing* states;

secessionist movements are still required first to establish their own existence (or at least a recognized state of belligerency) before they can apply for international legal rights.

Still, the law in this area is evolving. For instance, human rights have a new salience, even if pronouncements of "rights" in this area are often little more than statements of aspiration. (The Universal Declaration of Human Rights affirms the "right" of every person to "periodic holidays with pay" and "to a standard of living adequate for the health and well-being of himself and of his family, including . . . necessary social services . . . ."[26]) The Security Council *did* act to protect the Iraqi Kurds in 1991, finding a threat to "international peace and security." One author has argued that by 1975, when Morocco and Mauritania divided Western Sahara and Indonesia occupied East Timor, the invading states "admitted that the inhabitants . . . had a legal right to self-determination, and the dispute between them and their many critics at the United Nations was limited to the question of fact whether that right had been respected or violated."[27] Such a debate would have been inconceivable a century ago.

In the absence of clear legal rules, the international community will be forced to make its way largely by examining state practice. There is a good deal: Bangladesh, Cyprus, Irian Jaya, British Togoland, Cameroon, Mauritania, Goa, Fiji, Western Sahara, more.[28]

In sum, the legal response to ethnic demands for self-determination in the "postwar" period has been muddled, which is not necessarily to be disparaged. The life of the law, in Holmes's memorable observation, "has not been logic: it has been experience." Experience will now change, probably dramatically.

In large part this "postwar" legal muddle over claims to self-determination arose because they were too often assessed in terms of cold-war advantage/disadvantage. This was the context in which the major powers responded, for example, to the annexation of East Timor and the partition of Western Sahara, as well as the invasion of Angola. It happens I was United States representative at the U.N. when these events occurred. I defended a shameless American policy—Morocco and Indonesia were cold-war allies—with sufficient shamelessness. Only somewhat to be atoned for in a subsequent memoir:

A theme of our speeches throughout November had been that to corrupt the language of human rights—the language, that is, of Leo Strauss's "Modern Project," the language of "a society consisting of equal nations, each consisting of free and equal men and women"—would soon enough imperil the language of national rights also, and soon enough it did. In December, two fledgling nations were conquered or partitioned by their neighbors, while a third was invaded by Communist forces from half a world away. It would be gratifying to report that there were those who made some connection between what we said would happen and what now did happen, but there were none. This perhaps only confirmed our charge that the Charter was being drained of meaning.[29]

It may be noted that with the end of the cold war, the status of Western Sahara (which arguably has the right to decide whichever status it wishes) and of East Timor (which Indonesia seized) have returned to international councils, if only, in the case of Timor, by way of massacre.

Graham E. Fuller, sometime Vice-Chairman of the National Intelligence Council in the C.I.A. writes:

"Legitimate," of course, is the sticking point. How is "legitimacy" determined? Precedents for recent American policy are not encouraging. We have interpreted legitimacy to a great extent in accordance with our own Cold War interests. We tended to be sympathetic to movements that would weaken the U.S.S.R. and its allies, but to oppose movements that threatened our own allies. Latvians are fine, but not Palestinians. Tibetans thumbs up, but Kurds thumbs down. We were not entirely cynical, of course. We declined to support the Eritrean Liberation Front in Ethiopia—even when that front was waging war against the Marxist-Leninist regime of Mengistu Haile Mariam's Ethiopia. Our rationale was that separatist movements in Africa were uniquely dangerous, given the overall problems of tribalism and borders there.[30]

A cold-war nadir was reached in the 1973 Paris Peace Accords that ended American involvement in Vietnam. North Vietnam and the United States solemnly guaranteed that "the South Vietnamese people's right to self-determination is sacred, inalienable and shall be respected by all countries."[31] Further, it was decreed that the South Vietnamese people "shall decide themselves the political future of South Vietnam through genuinely free and democratic elections under international superivision."[32] The United States government never for one moment expected the Communist government of North Vietnam to abide by this treaty obligation. And when it did not, the United States made no significant protest, the "decent interval" having by then passed.

In truth, the war in Vietnam was much more an ideological war than the internal ethnic conflicts we are discussing here. The Vietnamese were divided over political systems. Even so the United States might have avoided becoming involved if we had only developed a sensitivity to ethnic conflict as *between* states nominally committed to the same cause of proletarian internationalism. In the early 1960s, the United States committed itself to war in Vietnam lest an ostensibly monolithic communist Soviet, Chinese, and Vietnamese column commence a long march down the littoral of Southeast Asia, hence presumedly up the Bay of Bengal to Calcutta. Had not Trotsky decreed that the road to Paris led through Calcutta? Well, yes: another of those predictions yet to come true. In any event, American policymakers were seemingly oblivious to the fact that these three peoples in their special ways hated one another. Even as we went to war against North Vietnam, its allies, the U.S.S.R. and the P.R.C., were virtually at war. The North Vietnamese had no more than taken the South when war, briefly, broke out with the Chinese. *As was foretold.* In a 1969 article in *World Politics,* Walker Connor laid out the exceptional ethnic heterogeneity of South Asia, including Vietnam, and the communist tactic of destabilizing multi-ethnic regimes by promising self-determination.[33] In Vietnam, as in China, a majority population occupies a relatively small proportion of the land area. In a resolution adopted at the First All-China Congress held in southern China in 1931, the Communists, noting the many minorities within then Nationalist China, pledged

that the Chinese Soviet Republic categorically and unconditionally recognizes the right of national minorities to self-determination. This means that in districts like Mongolia, Tibet, Sinkiang, Yunan, Kweichow, and others, where the majority of the population belongs to non-Chinese nationalities, the toiling masses of these nationalities shall have the right to determine for themselves whether they wish to leave the Chinese Soviet Republic and create their own independent state, or whether they wish to join the Union of Soviet Republics, or form an autonomous area inside the Chinese Soviet Republic.[34]

In 1935, Mao himself pledged to restore to the people of Inner Mongolia "the glory of the epoch of Genghis Khan" along with the "freedom and independence enjoyed by peoples such as those of Turkey, Poland, the Ukraine, and the Caucasus."[35] Sun Yat Sen had originally set forth the doctrine of China's five races: the Han, Tibetan, Uighers, Mongols, and Manchus. In 1948, the concept was emblazoned on the red flag of the People's Republic. A large star for the elder Han brother, with four attendant stars representing the others. Whereupon in 1949, the P.R.C. annexed Eastern Turkistan (or Sinkiang), and the following year, Tibet. In the process, the territory of the Red Chinese virtually doubled. Today the P.R.C. contains fifty-six so-called National Minority peoples, numbering some ninety million persons and inhabiting more than sixty percent of its territories.

Connor states that the Vietnamese Communists *did the same*. As Marxists they were part of a European political movement. In this sense only were the American policymakers correct in seeing communism as the issue. What we missed was the ethnic underlay, for the Vietnamese were scarcely the only people who lived in Vietnam. Again to cite Connor, Ho Chi Minh and his associates prior to the end of World War II "promised self-determination to all minorities within their sphere of power."[36] Later their supply lines to the south, their staging areas would be in just these interior regions. (Dien Bien Phu is in Hmong territory.) Regions of which the American mind knew little.

Again, and to yet again cite Horowitz: "The increasing prominence of ethnic loyalties is a development for which neither statesmen nor social scientists were adequately prepared. . . . The study of ethnic conflict has often been a grudging concession to something distasteful, largely because, especially in the West, ethnic affiliations have been in disrepute . . . . "[37] In Ainslee T. Embree's nice phrase, the great preoccupation of nineteenth-century Europe, the unification of Germany and Italy, suggested that throughout the world "unification into one great state represent[ed] the trend line of historical greatness."[38] In this respect, Marxism only added a subtext, a particular interpretation of the same trend. Nor was it all that wrong. Do we not observe the emergence of something very like a Western European state? There are other such trends. North America as an economic region. And yet there is also fragmentation, legitimated early in the century, now resumed.

The United States embraced the presumptively anti-colonial idea of self-determination in our own fit of absent-mindedness. There were wartime uses. But after a point, self-determination no longer seemed such a good idea. So many of the new states promptly turned Marxist or, as in the case of India, proclaimed themselves socialist with a Marxist bent.[39] What kind of gratitude was that?

The puzzlement was painfully in evidence at the United Nations. The United States had fashioned the new world order as much as possible in an American image.

WE THE PEOPLES OF THE UNITED NATIONS

If we were soon enough having troubles in the Security Council with the Soviet Union, the General Assembly remained at first "our" preserve, in the legitimate sense that those "United Nations" which had come together to wage war against fascism retained a clear majority in the "popular" branch of the world organization that had thereafter been created. But the new states had quite different views. The Non-Aligned Movement promptly aligned itself with the Soviet Union in international assemblies everywhere; most conspicuously the General Assembly in New York. What on earth was going on?

Not perhaps what we thought. I would offer the proposition that in the often incredibly heterogeneous former colonies that obtained independence following the Second World War, Marxism provided a rationale for rule by the dominant ethnic group; usually the most advanced group, sometimes merely the largest. Colonial students, typically children of elites, could pick up Marxism in Paris, Madrid, Lisbon. London also. New York for that matter. Take it home, nurture it to independence, sometimes fight for the real thing with a pure faith. (Think of the Chinese revolutionist, Old Gisors, in Malraux's *Man's Fate*. Think of Ho Chi Minh at the Paris Peace Conference.) But in the main and on the whole, Marxism with its Leninist exegesis of a one-party, all-powerful state which owned everything and ran everything, was curiously suited to the purposes of dominant castes the world over.

Consider the instance of India. Self-determination for India was a persistent wartime issue as between the United States and Britain; an insistent post-war aim of what became the senior partner in that special relationship. Independence came, and in no time the United States and India were on the verge of estrangement. The new nation, defiantly anti-western; both in cold-war terms and also in a singularly stultifying statism that permeated the society. But from an ethnic perspective the Indian choice appears curiously adaptive.

For a millennium prior to independence Indian elites had to deal with foreign rulers, first from central Asia, then from the North Atlantic. Jawaharlal Nehru once told the American ambassador John Kenneth Galbraith— only half-jokingly, as Galbraith recalls—that he was the last Englishman to rule India.[40] But foreign influences have come and gone, without greatly disturbing Hindu civilization with its central concept of *dharma*, a Sanskrit term, literally, that which is established. A civilization in which all social relations are decreed as duty, and defined by a priestly Brahminical caste, as for example, Kashmiri Brahmins such as the Nehrus, whose duty it is to govern. Embree sets the scene:

> The genius of the Brahmanical tradition is precisely its extraordinary continuity and its adherence to its own inner core of meaning, and it is this that provides the substance of the ideology that is a major factor in the unity of Indian civilization. . . . [S]ome items may be mentioned. One is a sense of order throughout the cosmos, linking all of its elements in a continuous and understandable pattern. Immediately related to this is the peculiar role of the possessor of knowledge, the Brahman, in maintaining this cosmic order. . . .

Closely linked to these concepts, as well as the others, is the sense of a hierarchical structure in which each entity occupies a necessary and logical place. The result, at least for those who live within it, is a wholly rational universe. To say that those who occupy the upper reaches of the hierarchy have, through the centuries, manipulated it for their own advantage would be to over-simplify the very complex dynamics of the historical process, but it is hard to escape the conclusion that while it is a simplification it is not a falsification. The Brahmans were not an aristocracy in the European sense, which combines blood lineages with economic and political power, but rather a class that identified with the ideology that provided rationality and coherence to society.[41]

Think: "cosmic order . . . rational universe . . . ideology . . . [providing] rationality and coherence." Is this not a Five Year Plan? Conceived, in accordance with the proper tests, and carried out, as is the proper order of the universe, by those whose role it is to perform such functions for society. A secularized Brahminism instantly settled on the new democracy, but given the fact of its being a democracy, claims on behalf of other groups began to be made with all the greater insistence as the fact of a new state offered all the greater rewards. And there were many more than a few such groups.

The Indian constitution, adopted in 1947, undertakes to secure "EQUALITY of status and of opportunity" for all citizens, but even so, includes a series of Articles, 330 to 342, making special provision for Anglo-Indians, Scheduled Castes, and Scheduled Tribes. In *The Constitution of India*, T. K. Tope observes that the Constitution had indeed accepted the principle of equality before the law: "communal electorates have been abolished."

But, "there are special provisions relating to certain classes."[42] Article 340 provided for a Backward Class Commission.[43] The first of these prepared a list of 2,399, of which 837 were classified as "most backward."[44] It is not difficult to see a spoils system at work here, but observe the capacity—and disposition—of human society to make caste distinctions. A 1980 Commission, named for its chairman, B. P. Mandal, recorded an unseeable caste called Purada Vannans. "They are not allowed to come out during day time because their sight is considered to be pollution. Some of these people who wash the clothes of other exterior castes working between midnight and day-break, were with difficulty persuaded to leave their houses to interview."[45]

Even so, the chairman of the first national commission, the "gentle Gandhian" Kaka Kalekar, had second thoughts. His work finished, he drew back. In a forwarding letter to the President, he appears to have rejected the whole concept.

Being convinced that the upper castes among the Hindus have to atone for the neglect of which they were guilty towards the "lower" classes, I was prepared to recommend to Government that all special help should be given only to the backward classes and even the poor and the deserving among the upper classes may be safely kept out from the benefit of this special help. My eyes were however opened to the dangers of suggesting remedies on the caste basis when I discovered that it is going to have a most unhealthy effect on the Muslim and Christian sections of the nation. . . .

This was a rude shock and it drove me to the conclusion that the remedies we suggested were worse than the evil we were out to combat.[46]

Even so, an ever more elaborate system of "special help" and government planning took hold.

By the start of the fifth decade of Indian independence, a process of demystification had begun. Indian scholars began to associate *caste* with *ethnicity*. In an essay, "Ethnicity, Democracy, and Development in India," Jyotirindra Das Gupta wrote in 1988: "Planning may simply conceal and rationalize a pattern of ethnic domination that by its nature may evoke opposing forces of resentment and generate demands for access to the club of dominance and advantage."[47] In 1991 a young scholar, Sanjay Yadav, presented a paper at Queen Elizabeth House at Oxford entitled: "The Mandal Milestone: Class and Caste in the 1990's." Note the echo of Dollard's work.

When the Mandal Commission submitted its report in 1980, Indira Gandhi, as Prime Minister, simply filed it away. However, a subsequent Prime Minister, V. P. Singh, brought it forward in 1989 in a national election that in turn brought riots to the streets of major cities with young Brahmins, seemingly facing the prospect of losing places at universities, immolating themselves. The next government dropped the subject, but the issue does not go away. Yadav (the name of an agricultural caste much beloved of Krishna) makes the point with admirable directness:

In India caste functions as a quasi-ethnicity. Castes may be appropriately called ethnic or sub-ethnic formations for they function in ways that are equivalent to the ways that nations and nationalities function elsewhere. Indian castes all have their subjective histories, their notions of defeat and triumph, failure and success, notions that are the life-blood of nationalities.[48]

He goes further to attempt to quantify the matter:

Though issues about class and caste have a long history of debate surrounding them, it is nevertheless necessary to first clarify some meanings. The argument that caste provides the basis for social stratification in India implies that rich, well-to-do, socially and politically influential individuals belong principally to the upper castes, especially the priestly castes. This argument admits that some individuals from even the lowest castes can be found in the upper economic stratum of Indian society. It is maintained, however, that in the main caste correlates with class; that upper castes, less than twenty percent of Indian society, constitute the dominant economic class and that, conversely, lower castes, constitute the economically deprived mass. Advocates of his view do not normally put a statistical figure on the extent of the correlation, but it would seem that they see a correlation ranging from .7 to .9.[49]

In the 1980s, the first seemingly sustainable opposition party emerged to challenge Congress, the party of independence, the Bharatiya Janata Party. (*Bharat* being the Sanskrit term for India; *Janata* meaning people.) The B.J.P. is unabashedly a Hindu party. Its edges are softened by the assertion that *everyone* living in the subcontinent is a Hindu, whether or not they realize this, and all are welcome. Of which there is considerable truth, Hinduism not being a doctrinal creed such as Judaism or Christianity. On the other hand, the B.J.P. was distinctive for asserting what might be called a class interest, that of the merchant and business castes. To many B.J.P. activists socialism clearly means Brahminism. A market economy would be in the hands of *their* castes. An

editorial in the *Times of India* in January 1992 entitled
"Caste in a Mould," lamented that "The class content
[of the B.J.P. program] is not covered up by the caste
idiom." Of Mr. Laloo Prasad Yadav, chief minister of the
ever-stricken province of Bihar, the *Times* goes on:

With the social chasm widening, it is not certain how long Mr.
Yadav can carry on such intermediacy. His over-emphasis on
caste rather than class as the primary factor of social change also
does not make the situation better. The least he and others
entrusted with the responsibility of governance can do is to
stick to implementing the law. Even that would be a major step
in preventing the brutal attacks on poor and helpless
Harijans.[50]

But the dynamic of caste will not be denied, notably in
Dollard's matrix of caste *and* class. The problem for
India, as for every sizable state in the region, is to
maintain unity in the face of ethnic strife. "Unity in
diversity" was the original theme of Indian patriots. The
founders of the modern Indian state saw themselves as
modern, secular, liberals. Others saw differently. Not
least Mohammed Ali Jinnah, who has perhaps been
unfairly blamed for partition in 1947. It has been said
that he saw, or thought he saw, "majority rule as Hindu
rule and as a way of making Hindu and Indian into
convertible terms."[51] In Embree's nice summation,
under the majority represented by the pre-independence
Congress leadership, "Secularism, socialism, and Brah-
manism marched under the strange ideological device of
the *chakra* which Gandhi had emblazoned on the banner
of Congress nationalism."[52] A half century and more
have passed; rivers of blood have run to the sea or seeped

into the sand; the point is just beginning to be understood.

What is to be done? Not, perhaps, a great deal. Toward the end of his life, Harold Isaacs, the most vibrant of men, grew near to despair. In 1981, returning from a visit to his beloved Israel, he would write that it had become "a bleak place, falling into the hands of nationalist-tribal zealots hand-in-hand with medieval-religious-fanatic zealots."[53] It will end a very different place from that imagined by "those earlier socialist-Zionist-zealots who started it all nearly a century ago, and yet, in that terrible way the logic of politics has, the one perhaps has to lead to the other."[54] American "myopias" precluded any helpful role there or elsewhere.[55] And then this in 1984: "I am more, not less, at a loss than I have been for years in spotting any bright patches in the gloom."[56]

For the American government a decade later, there was difficulty spotting anything, bright or otherwise. Foreign policy was now in the hands of what Fukuyama calls "hyper-realists," those who "believe that international life is the relentless, amoral clash of national interests and that America should be guided by mere balance-of-power considerations."[57] If Dr. Kissinger had been the "most articulate theorist of hyper-realism," nonetheless, the Bush administration's "solicitousness of the aging Communists in Beijing and . . . pullback from full victory in Iraq are perhaps the best examples of hyper-realism in practice."[58] This may be harsh, and yet American policy seemed at times incapable of conceptualizing a world in which states break up. As regards ethnicity in international politics, American policy persisted in getting it wrong. Even as the Slovenes and Croats were declaring their independence and a Serbian-dominated army was on the move, Secretary of State James A. Baker III was insisting that "The United States continues to recognize and support the territorial integrity of Yugoslavia . . . . "⁵⁹

American policy changed, but always in response to events, rather than anticipation of them. (Was it *that* difficult to see that Yugoslavia was coming apart?) Similarly, on March 11, 1990, the Lithuanian parliament voted to restore Lithuanian independence. It received no encouragement from the United States despite a fifty-year policy of refusing to recognize the annexation of the Baltic states by the Soviet Union. The United States waited until September 2, 1991 to establish diplomatic relations with the Baltic states, after more than thirty other states had already done so.

On August 1, 1991, the President of the United States journeyed to Kiev to address the Supreme Soviet of the Ukrainian Soviet Socialist Republic. The Union of Soviet Socialist Republics was already over. Done. Finished. And the American President's message? Don't be hasty. Don't succumb to the snares and delusions of "independence" and "suicidal nationalism." Would that Lord North had summoned such eloquence: "Freedom is not the same as independence. Americans will not support those who seek independence in order to replace a far-off tyranny with a local despotism. They will not aid those who promote a suicidal nationalism based upon ethnic hatred."⁶⁰ William Safire of the *New York Times* promptly labeled this Bush's "Chicken Kiev" speech, but it was more than a speech. The American government, as far back as the 1970s, had missed completely the onset of instability in the region. In a remarkable article in *Foreign Affairs* in the fall of 1991, Admiral Stansfield Turner, who had been Director of Central Intelligence under President Jimmy Carter, so stated in the most forceful terms. On his watch, too.

We should not gloss over the enormity of this failure to forecast the magnitude of the Soviet crisis. . . . I never heard a suggestion from the CIA . . . that numerous Soviets recognized a growing systemic economic problem.

Today we hear some revisionist rumblings that the CIA did in fact see the Soviet collapse emerging after all. . . . On this one, the corporate view missed by a mile.[61]

This ought to have given "cover" to the Bush administration, which only came to office early in 1989, but to the contrary. In 1992, President Bush's Director of Central Intelligence, Robert M. Gates, told the Foreign Policy Association in New York that the Agency had looked into the matter with great care and found nothing to fault in its performance. Mind, "only in early 1989 did we begin to think the entire edifice might well collapse."[62]

Again, the inadequacy is not to be ascribed to one President or one administration. There has been and continues to be an inadequate understanding of what has made the world turn upside down. I end about where I began. There was enough of a knowledge base, both theoretical and practical, to make possible a sufficiently accurate anticipation as to what the present era would look like. Let us hold firm to that. The world does not defy understanding; and what can be understood can sometimes be modified.

In the next fifty years there will be, what, fifty new countries? One hundred fifty? The International Geographical Union has already established a special Commission on the World Political Map, anticipating primal fissury. Most new states will appear in Africa and Asia. (Some in North America? Possibly.)

We can say with an equal order of confidence that most of these new states will be badly off, not least from the point of view of ethnic homogeneity. Nor will they have much in the way of a civic culture. If Max Weber could lament that Otto von Bismarck had left a German nation "totally without any political education," what may we expect by way of political education in the breakaway nationalisms that will establish independent states in the period ahead?[63] Not much by way of constabulary, less by way of judiciary. And, withal that socialism is out of favor for the moment, we should not expect very much by way of free enterprise in states created for the purpose of giving one or another ethnic group a realm of its own.

All this argues that the larger states and the various associations of states—and, clearly, the United Nations itself—need to set about fashioning responses to con-flicts concerning "self-determination." The U.N. has little to commend itself save the fact that it is there, and the Charter purports to set out the rules. These will not be pretty events, and expect a fair degree of compassion fatigue on the part of the donors and the peacekeepers. It will also be necessary for the United States and also, even, the democracies of Western Europe to reconsider what Reinhold Niebuhr once called "The Myth of Democratic

Universality," the idea that democracy is a "universal option for all nations." Civil rights preceded political rights in the West, and this may be the most that can be hoped for in many of the new states. Niebuhrian realism was not much in favor in the later stages of the cold war, but all things come round. Americans could usefully contribute a measure of Madisonian realism to what will be a new era of constitution-building in regions around the world. Stratified systems of governance, call it federalism where appropriate, are clearly a necessity if any order is to emerge from the proximate confusion.

With any luck—and why not?—there will also be examples of successful adaptation, compromise, evolution. Even as night descended once again on the Balkans, in the Alps not far away Austria and Italy reached an amicable resolution concerning the status of the South Tirol, a German speaking region seized by Italians in 1918. Further West the Olympic Games commenced in Barcelona. Advertisements in *The Economist* welcomed visitors to Catalonia, "a country in Spain with its own culture, language and identity."[64]

Not every separation, devolution, *ad hoc* accommodation will be without grief. But humor and intellect help. In the aftermath of the 1992 elections in the former Czechoslovakia, it became clear that the Slovaks had determined to form an independent state. Vaclav Havel, as President of the already bifurcated "Czech and Slovak Federal Republic," serenely left office, the while suggesting he might return as head of what would be a new Czech Republic. More likely, he speculated, "the Czech-Moravian-Silesian Federal and Federative Republic."[65]

The United States will need more than a few of these

virtues, and will know more than it has known of grief. Grief of a different kind. We have known the grief of caste-imposed subjection; we must now expect caste retaliation. It is already there, on the streets. In so far as the Lord loves the United States, this otherwise ominous evolution is complicated by the huge immigration of the 1970s and 1980s. Race—black-white—has been a primal division in American life, but never the sole division. It will now be dissolved further by the vast numbers of new Hispanic- and Asian-Americans (among others), with some surprising role reversals that many of the principals have, as yet, barely noticed. Thus, at any given moment in the last decade of the twentieth century, something like half the ten largest cities in the United States will have a black mayor or a black police chief or both. To the million legal immigrants in New York City (to which add, say, half a million illegal immigrants), this is the "power structure," with all the attendant tensions.

These tensions are exacerbated, as theory and practice predict, by spreading patterns of group preferences silting up the interstices of municipal government. This is nothing new; informal patterns of preference and discrimination are indigenous to big-city government in the United States. What *is* new is that they should be mandated by law, which law once nominally forbade them. The Civil Rights Act of 1982 sought to strengthen minority representation in Congress, but provided "That nothing in this [act] establishes a right to have members of a *protected class* elected in numbers equal to their proportion in the population" (my emphasis). But came the next decennial census and the attendant congressional redistricting, and this is precisely the right that was asserted. "Protected classes" had entered the vocabulary of American election law. What are now known as "majority-minority" congressional districts came into being during the reapportionment.

Predictably, things didn't always work out as the new interpretation of the statute prescribed. In the summer of 1992, a headline in *Roll Call*, the newspaper of Capitol Hill, reported the results of a primary contest in Houston: "Green, an Anglo, Wins Latino-Majority Seat."[66] Almost alone, Representative John Lewis of Georgia, who distinguished himself in the civil rights struggles of the 1960s, has distinguished himself yet again by protesting that the new "majority-minority" districts the courts now insist on are the equivalent of the black townships of South Africa.

Such misery, wholly self-inflicted, has only just begun. The implications are clear enough. Not least in presenting ourselves as a model to a world which will continue to be more often hostile than admiring. What we have to offer is our standards.

The rest of the world, much of the rest of the world, can in turn offer warnings. Horowitz has been setting forth careful, factual analyses of "preferential policies" in various societies. They are, he seems to conclude, with the rarest exception, the surest formula for "interethnic" conflict. From independence forward, for example, governments of the Buddhist Sinhalese majority enacted preferences of one or another kind for the Sinhalese, notably in the civil service, the military, and the police. In 1977 the Buddhist government of J. R. Jayewardene, on the grounds of equity, began to reverse or modify these preferences, setting aside spots for the minority Tamils.[67] Terror descended on the land. On November 3, 1984, along with Senator Howard H. Baker, Jr., I represented the United States Congress in the United States delegation at the funeral of Indian Prime Minister Indira Gandhi who had been assassinated by her Sikh guards. At the end of the day our delegation met with Jayewardene, who was also in New Delhi. The murder of his friend by ethnic terrorists was too much for him. Not favored in his features, even so an intense truthfulness shone through. To have watched the face of this intelligent, honorable man describing Buddhist mobs throwing Tamils alive into bonfires in the capital of Colombo is to have sensed anguish beyond words. In time Tamils would assassinate Rajiv Gandhi, Indira's son and heir. Patterns.

Scholars also need to attend to successes. The partitions that didn't happen. The strife that went away. The multi-ethnic societies that seem to work. (As New York City was doing when Glazer and I first wrote about it; as it does not seem to be doing today.) Years ago, for example, Milton Gordon pointed out that in 1818 Irish charitable organizations in New York and Philadelphia had sought the aid of the Federal government to provide land in the west on which to settle indigent Gaels.[68] Not a chance, said Congress. Wisely. The United States, in the main, has been spared autonomous regions, bantustans, enclaves. (Reservations, yes. Our worst mistake or worst dilemma, as you wish.) Such has to be the *policy* of a nation of immigrants. But as we proclaim—and oh, do we proclaim—the richness of the immigrant heritage, we do well to consider the richness of the cultures from which it came. The great economic unions going forward in Europe and elsewhere put at risk the richness of the cultures that for ages have protected themselves behind castle walls and tariff barriers. (Do we await a "European" cheese?) The instinctive response to insurrection such as that in the Balkans will be to suppress distinctiveness, to drown it in subsidy and choke it with regulation.

There is an alternative. Niebuhr warns of collective egotism, Auden of collective egoism; however termed, it readily enough becomes destructive. But there is nothing wrong—everything right—with an intelligent, responsible self-respect, even self-regard. The challenge is to make the world safe for and from ethnicity, safe for just those differences which large assemblies, democratic or otherwise, will typically attempt to suppress. The idea deserves attention. As does the whole question of sovereignty. Lawyers speak of property rights as actually a collection of rights. Clearly, in this sense sovereignty has become more permeable. Increasingly the United Nations finds it possible to intervene in ethnic conflicts citing, as in the case of a Balkan war crimes panel resolution, "obligations under international humanitarian law." There have not as yet been any dramatic results, but idea has heft. The horror does not go away, and an international community will in fact ask itself just how much horror can be looked upon with indifference, or at least inaction. To which the answer, of course, is plenty. But a large capacity to tolerate atrocity does not imply an unlimited capacity. Civilizations with claims to universal values, do, in general, try to uphold them, if only after a point.

For the moment the more pressing matter is simply to contain the risk, to restrain the tendency to hope for too much, either of altruism or of common sense. Pandaemonium was inhabited by creatures quite convinced that the great Satan had their best interests at heart. Poor little devils.

NOTES

INTRODUCTION

1. Walker Connor, "From Tribe to Nation," *History of European Ideas,* vol. 13, no. 1/2 (1991), 6 (emphasis in the original).
2. Walker Connor, "When is a Nation?", *Ethnic and Racial Studies,* vol. 13, no. 1 (Jan. 1990), 99.
3. Eugen Weber, *Peasants into Frenchmen: The Modernization of Rural France, 1870–1914* (Stanford, Calif.: Stanford University Press, 1976), 67.
4. Connor, "When is a Nation?", 99.
5. Transcript of an address by Mikhail Gorbachev to the Congress of the United States, May 14, 1992, 8–9.
6. *The Economist,* Aug. 10, 1991, 9.
7. *New York Times,* Nov. 22, 1991, A30.
8. *The Economist,* 35.
9. Ibid. 37–8.
10. Daniel P. Moynihan, *On the Law of Nations* (Cambridge, Mass.: Harvard University Press, 1990).
11. Transcript of a news conference by President Bush, *New York Times,* Aug. 23, 1990, A16.
12. F. H. Hinsley, *Nationalism and the International System* (London: Hodder & Stoughton, 1973).
13. Elie Halévy, *The World Crisis of 1914–1918* (Oxford: Clarendon Press, 1930), 37, quoted in Hinsley, 12.
14. Quoted ibid. 14 n.
15. Bernadotte Schmitt, *The Origins of the First World War* (London: Routledge & Kegan Paul, 1958), 6–7, quoted in ibid. 12.
16. While the four members of the Commonwealth—Australia, Canada, New Zealand and South Africa—did not become *de jure* independent until after 1914, at that time they did enjoy *de facto* independence. Conversely, Bhutan has been technically independent since 1914, but was effectively a British protectorate for

part of that period. Portugal and Costa Rica have not suffered violent revolutions, but both states have had their governments changed by military coups. Although Liechtenstein was perhaps technically independent in 1914, its highest government officials and Supreme Court were located in Austria. It was not until 1918 that newly amended electoral laws produced a fundamental shift in Liechtenstein's orientation toward self-government. Iceland achieved a degree of home rule in 1874, but did not become internally self-governing until 1918 and waited until 1944 for full independence from Denmark. Several states which would otherwise gain admission to this exclusive club based on internal stability—such as the Netherlands and Denmark—have suffered foreign occupations during which normal self-government was in large part suspended.

17. A revised edition which does contain a definition of "ethnicity" was published in the United States as *The Harper Dictionary of Modern Thought* (New York: Harper & Row, 1988) (2nd edn.), 285

18. Donald L. Horowitz, *Ethnic Groups in Conflict* (Berkeley, Calif.: University of California Press, 1985), p. xi. Connor describes the origins of the terms "nation" and "ethnic":

> *Nation* derives from the past participle of the Latin verb *nasci* ("to be born"), and hence the Latin noun *nationem*, which connoted breed or race. *Ethnic* is derived from the closest equivalent to *nationem* in ancient Greek, *ethnos*, and *thus ethnic* group, properly used, also refers, in Max Weber's words, to "those human groups that entertain a subjective belief in their common descent."

Walker Connor, "The Nation and Its Myth," (unpub. MS), 22 n., to be pub. in the *International Journal of Comparative Sociology*.

19. Hinsley, *Nationalism and the International System*, 20.

20. Transcript of remarks by Boris N. Yeltsin, President of the Russian Federation, before a Joint Session of the Congress of the United States, June 17, 1992.

21. Here is the passage in all its glory.

> "You an' me, Hinnissy, has got to bring on this here Anglo-Saxon 'lieance. An Anglo-Saxon, Hinnissy, is a German that's forgot who was his parents. They're a lot iv thim in this

counthry. There must be as manny as two in Boston: they'se wan up in Maine, an' another lives at Bogg's Ferry in New York State, an' dhrives a milk wagon. Mack is an Anglo-Saxon. His folks come fr'm th' County Armagh, an' their naytional Anglo-Saxon hymn is 'O'Donnell Aboo.' Teddy Rosenfelt is another Anglo-Saxon. An' I'm an Anglo-Saxon. I'm wan iv th' hottest Anglo-Saxons that iver come out iv Anglo-Saxony. Th' name iv Dooley has been th' proudest Anglo-Saxon name in th' County Roscommon f'r many years.

"Schwartzmeister is an Anglo-Saxon, but he doesn't know it, an' won't till some wan tells him. Pether Bowbeen down be th' Frinch church is formin' th' Circle Francaize Anglo-Saxon club, an' me ol' frind Dominigo that used to boss th' Ar-rchey R-road wagon whin Callaghan had th' sthreet conthract will march at th' head iv th' Dago Anglo-Saxons whin th' time comes. There ar-re twenty thousan' Rooshian Jews at a quarther a vote in th' Sivinth Ward; an', ar-rmed with rag hooks, they'd be a tur-r-ble thing f'r anny inimy iv th' Anglo-Saxon 'lieance to face. Th' Bohemians an' Pole Anglo-Saxons may be a little slow in wakin' up to what th' pa-apers calls our common hurtage, but ye may be sure they'll be all r-right whin they're called on. We've got together an Anglo-Saxon 'lieance in this wa-ard, an' we're goin' to ilict Sarsfield O'Brien prisidint, Hugh O'Neill Darsey vice-prisidint, Robert Immitt Clancy sicrety, an' Wolfe Tone Malone three-asurer. O'Brien'll be a good wan to have. He was in the Fenian r-raid, an' his father carrid a pike in forty-eight. An' he's in th' Clan. Besides, he has a sthrong pull with th' Ancient Ordher iv Anglo-Saxon Hibernyans.

"I tell ye, whin th' Clan an' th' Sons iv Sweden an' th' Banana Club an' th' Circle Francaize an' th' Pollacky Benivolent Society an' th' Rooshian Sons of Dinnymite an' th' Benny Brith an' th' Coffee Clutch that Schwartzmeister r-runs an' th' Tur-rnd'ye-mind an' th' Holland society an' th' Afro-Americans an' th' other Anglo-Saxons begin f'r to raise their Anglo-Saxon battlecry, it'll be all day with th' eight or nine people in th' wurruld that has th' misfortune iv not bein' brought up Anglo-Saxons."

Finley Peter Dunne, *Mr. Dooley in Peace and in War* (Boston: Small, Maynard, 1898), 34–5. Note the fluidity of many of these terms. Bohemians would soon become Czechs and form an alliance with American Slovaks sufficient to proclaim the independence of Czechoslovakia in Pittsburgh on May 30, 1918.

22. *New York Times*, July 26, 1992, sec. 4, 5.
23. Martin Ridge, "Frederick Jackson Turner and His Ghost: The Writing of Western History," *Proceedings of the American Antiquarian Society*, vol. 101, pt. I (1991), 66.
24. Ibid.
25. Quoted ibid.
26. A *casus belli* was required, of course, and for Wilson it was the violation of the freedom of the seas. This was Wilson's intellectual rationale for choosing sides and it is possible that he was unaware at a conscious level of any other basis. I have discussed Wilson's legal rationale at some length elsewhere. See Moynihan, *On the Law of Nations*, 33–7.
27. Charles Krauthammer, "America's Case of the Sulks," *Washington Post*, Jan. 19, 1992, C7.
28. *New York Times*, Jan. 26, 1992, A12.
29. *New York Times*, Dec. 23, 1991, A1.
30. *The Economist*, Dec. 21, 1991, 45.
31. *New York Times*, May 24, 1992, sect. 4, 1.
32. Ibid.
33. *New York Times*, May 26, 1992, A6. These matters much concern Americans. In the spring of 1992 a march in Washington, D.C., endorsed by the U. S. Conference of Mayors in support of increased federal aid to cities and to children, drew some 35,000 participants according to the National Park Service. A few weeks later a march by Greek Americans to insist that the newly independent province of Macedonia, in what had been Yugoslavia, not be allowed to call itself "Macedonia," attracted some 20,000 participants.
34. William Pfaff, "It's Now or Never for the West to Intervene in Bosnia," *Chicago Tribune*, May 24, 1992, sect. 4, 3.
35. Quoted ibid.
36. *Chicago Tribune*, May 24, 1992, sect. 4, 1.
37. Serge Schmemann, "Ethnic Battles Flaring in Former Soviet Fringe," *New York Times*, May 24, 1992, 7.

38. Ibid.
39. *New York Times*, May 26, 1992, A7.
40. We are now seeing the eruption of a full-fledged struggle between Hazara Shiites and Pathan Sunnis in Afghanistan: "Militiamen loyal to the Islamic caretaker government tried to halt street battles between rival ethnic militias. . . . Fighters of an ethnic Hazara militia battled a Pathan-led group. The Hazaras are Shiite Muslims with links to Iran; the rival Ittihad-i-Islami is backed by Saudis of the Sunni sect of Islam." *Washington Post*, June 6, 1992, A17.
41. See Rebecca West, *Black Lamb and Grey Falcon: A Journey through Yugoslavia* (New York: Viking Press, 1941).
42. *New York Times*, May 26, 1992, A6.
43. *The Economist*, May 23, 1992, 53.
44. David L. Sills and Robert K. Merton (eds.), *International Encyclopedia of the Social Sciences* (New York: Macmillan, 1991), vol. 19, p. 79.
45. Nathan Glazer, *The Social Basis of American Communism* (New York: Harcourt, Brace & World, 1961).
46. Meg Greenfield, "The Great Scott Syndrome," *Washington Post*, May 18, 1992, A21.
47. William Rees-Mogg, "The Sheriff Fiddles while the Town Burns," *Independent*, May 4, 1992, 17.
48. Solomon F. Bloom, "The Peoples of my Hometown: Before Nationalism Crushed Rumania's Design for Living," *Commentary*, Apr. 1947, 329.
49. Ibid. 335.
50. Harold R. Isaacs, *Idols of the Tribe: Group Identity and Political Change* (New York: Harper & Row, 1975), 215.

CHAPTER 1: ETHNICITY AS A DISCIPLINE

1. Milton M. Gordon, "Toward a General Theory of Racial and Ethnic Group Relations," in Nathan Glazer and Daniel P. Moynihan (eds.), *Ethnicity: Theory and Experience* (Cambridge, Mass.: Harvard University Press, 1975), 88.
2. Donald Horowitz, *Ethnic Groups in Conflict* (Berkeley, Calif.: University of California Press, 1985), 87.
3. Quoted ibid. 88. Social Darwinists of the late 19th century tended also to see religion as a characteristic of the early stages of

sociocultural evolution, and destined to disappear with advancement.
4. Ibid.
5. E. J. Hobsbawm, *Nations and Nationalism Since 1780: Programme, Myth, Reality* (Cambridge: Cambridge University Press, 1990), 183.
6. John Dollard, *Caste and Class in a Southern Town* (Madison, Wisc.: University of Wisconsin Press, 1988) (foreword by Daniel P. Moynihan).
7. Richard Hofstadter, *The Paranoid Style in American Politics and Other Essays* (New York: Alfred A. Knopf, 1965), 3.
8. Ibid. 22.
9. Nathan Glazer and Daniel P. Moynihan, *Beyond the Melting Pot: The Negroes, Puerto Ricans, Jews, Italians, and Irish of New York City* (Cambridge, Mass.: M.I.T. Press, 1970) (2nd edn.), 315.
10. Daniel Bell, "Nationalism or Class?—Some Questions on the Potency of Political Symbols," *The Student Zionist*, May 1947, 7.
11. Ibid. 11.
12. Ibid. Walker Connor writes of an even earlier example of the predictive power attainable through appreciation of the power of ethnic attachments:

The theme of this essay has been that recent ethnonational developments within Western Europe can be viewed as a sequential, evolutionary step in the extension of the force field of nationalism. Recalling again the surprise occasioned by the factual undermining of those two postwar pillars of scholarship on Western Europe (the obsolescence of nationalism and the absence of multinational states), consider the following passage by Carlton Hayes: "One striking feature of the period's nationalist agitation, obviously, was that it affected and widely publicized a number of European peoples that had not previously been supposed to have national consciousness or political aspirations. Another of its features, even more startling, was its quickened tempo and fiercer manifestation among . . . peoples already known to be nationalist." By peoples "not previously been supposed to have national consciousness," Hayes was indeed referring to Basque, Breton, Catalan, Flemish, and the like. The passage, however, was written not in the 1970's but in 1941; not to describe Western

Europe of the 1960's and 1970's, but of the 1870's, 1880's, and 1890's. The point is that the more sensitive literature on nationalism written in the prewar period did contain valuable clues to what might be expected to occur within Western Europe as nationalism further evolved. As early as 1926, for example, Hayes warned of troubles between ethnonational groups within Belgium and Switzerland, "despite the artificial attempts to promote a sense of social solidarity, akin to nationality, among all the Swiss and among all the Belgians." He also referred to "the budding little nationalisms of Icelanders, Catalans, Provencals, Basques, Wends, White Russians (Belorussians), Manx, and Maltese.

Walker Connor, "Ethnonationalism in the First World: The Present in Historical Perspective," in Milton J. Esman (ed.), *Ethnic Conflict in the Western World* (Ithaca, N.Y.: Cornell University Press, 1975), 43–4.

13. The notion that Jewish and Arab workers would unite against common class enemies seems hard to credit after 45 years of bloody history in the Middle East, but it was held by many: "Some socialist Zionists, like Ber Borochov, believed that Jewish and Arab workers would together rise up against the exploitative *effendis*, and that class solidarity between Jewish and Arab workers would overwhelm the cultural and ethnic differences between them." (Adam M. Garfinkle, "On the Origin, Meaning, Use and Abuse of a Phrase," *Middle Eastern Studies*, vol. 27, no. 4 (Oct. 1991), 542.) Charles Blitzer points to Borochov's 1905 essay "The National Question and the Class Struggle" as a "marvelous example of the notion that class would triumph over ethnicity." (Charles Blitzer to Daniel P. Moynihan, June 11, 1992.) The essay is reprinted in Arthur Hertzberg (ed.), *The Zionist Idea* (New York: Atheneum, 1969), 355–60.

14. Daniel P. Moynihan, "Will Russia Blow Up?," *Newsweek*, Nov. 19, 1979, 144.

15. White House meeting with leaders of the United Nicaraguan Opposition (Mar. 3, 1986), quoted in *Washington Post*, Mar. 4, 1986, A21.

16. For a full account of these events, see Daniel P. Moynihan with Suzanne Weaver, *A Dangerous Place* (Boston: Little, Brown, 1978).

17. G. A. Res. 3379 (1975), in UNGA *Official Records: 30th Session*, suppl. 34 (Doc. A-10034), 83–4.
18. Moynihan with Weaver, *A Dangerous Place*, 249.
19. Murray Feshbach and Stephen Rapawy, "Soviet Population and Manpower Trends and Policies," in Joint Economic Committee, *Soviet Economy in a New Perspective*, 94th Cong., 2nd Ses., Oct. 14, 1976 (Washington, D.C.: Government Printing Office, 1976), 113.
20. Ibid. 116.
21. Christopher Davis and Murray Feshbach, *Rising Infant Mortality in the U.S.S.R. in the 1970's*, series P-95, no. 74 (Washington, D.C.: Bureau of the Census, U.S. Department of Commerce, 1980), 1.
22. See Raymond Augustine Bauer, *The New Man in Soviet Psychology* (Cambridge, Mass.: Harvard University Press, 1952).
23. Milton M. Gordon to Daniel P. Moynihan, July 28, 1992.
24. Daniel P. Moynihan, "Will Russia Blow Up?," 144. It should be recorded that there were limits to my confidence. Upon being appointed Godkin Lecturer at Harvard University for the academic year 1984–5, I resolved to give the requisite three lectures on this subject. I would announce the impending dissolution of the Soviet Union and analyze the event from an ethnic perspective. Noting in particular the plight of Soviet Jews, desperate to escape to Israel or *anywhere*, but imprisoned by an autocracy which understood all too well what it implied that anyone, much less a large and educated group, should want to leave what was, after all, their home. But on second thought, I asked myself how I would respond to the inevitable question from the inevitable former colleague who would ask when, since leaving Cambridge, had I found time to learn Russian, and hence knew so much about the U.S.S.R.! I lectured on family policy instead.
25. *Congressional Record*, 96th Cong., 2nd Sess., vol. 126, pt. 1, p. 35.
26. Published in Daniel P. Moynihan, *Came the Revolution: Argument in the Reagan Era* (New York: Harcourt, Brace, Jovanovich, 1988), 190–1.
27. Quoted in *Buffalo News*, Oct. 15, 1984, C4.

28. Nathan Glazer and Daniel P. Moynihan, in Alan Bullock, Oliver Stallybrass, and Stephen Trombley (eds.), *The Harper Dictionary of Modern Thought* (New York: Harper & Row, 1988) (2nd edn.), 285.
29. Daniel P. Moynihan, "Reagan's Doctrine and the Iran Issue," *New York Times*, Dec. 21, 1986, E19.
30. *Congressional Record*, 100th Cong., 1st Sess., vol. 133, no. 18, p. S13474.
31. Richard M. Nixon, *The Real War* (New York: Warner Books, 1980), 1–3.
32. Max M. Kampelman to Daniel P. Moynihan, Dec. 3, 1991.
33. Theodore Draper, "Getting Irangate Straight," *New York Review of Books*, Oct. 8, 1987, 47.
34. John Lewis Gaddis, *The United States and the End of the Cold War: Implications, Reconsiderations, Provocations* (New York: Oxford University Press, 1992), p. vii.
35. Transcript of remarks by Henry A. Kissinger to the Nixon Library Conference, Mar. 12, 1992. In fairness, Dr. Kissinger later wrote me to say, "I stand corrected. Your crystal ball was better than mine." Henry A. Kissinger to Daniel P. Moynihan, Apr. 2, 1992.
36. Hélène Carrère d'Encausse, *Decline of an Empire: the Soviet Socialist Republics in Revolt* (New York: Newsday Books, 1979), 273.
37. Ibid. 274. Another celebrated example of predicting the collapse of the Soviet empire is Andrei Amalrik's *Will the Soviet Union Survive Until 1984?* (New York: Harper & Row, 1970). Amalrik keenly discerns and vividly describes the ideological hollowness of the Soviet regime during the Brezhnev era, but does not have a great deal to say about ethnic conflict as a vehicle for change, other than the dangers of Russian nationalism. Significantly, however, he possesses an intellectual's appreciation for the importance of doctrine and the problem that a "crisis of faith" will pose for an ideological regime: "I have no doubt that this great Eastern Slav empire, created by Germans, Byzantines and Mongols, has entered the last decades of its existence. . . . Marxist doctrine has delayed the break-up of the Russian Empire—the third Rome—but does not possess the power to prevent it." (Ibid. 65)

Amalrik's thesis in sum is that a weak and passive, but growing, middle class, with an interest in establishing the rule of law is being resisted by a weak and passive regime. In these circumstances, a fall in the standard of living—which Amalrik considered entirely possible, if not likely—would have explosive results. He concludes that the probable response of the regime would be nationalist rhetoric and—his key prediction—a war with Communist China. His prediction of the result (even if the vehicle of change was other than what he expected) *is* remarkable in its similarity to what actually occurred: "It is also possible that the 'middle class' [Amalrik's term for the pro-rule of law and democracy forces] will prove strong enough to keep control in its own hands. In that case, the granting of independence to the various Soviet nationalities will come about peacefully and some sort of federation will be created, similar to the British Commonwealth or the European Economic Community. . . . It is even possible that the Ukraine, the Baltic Republics and European Russia will enter a Pan-European federation as independent units." (Ibid. 64–5.)

38. *Handbook of Economic Statistics, 1980* (Washington, D.C.:Central Intelligence Agency, 1980), table 9, p. 24 (Soviet G.N.P. at 62% of U.S. G.N.P. in 1975); *Handbook of Economic Statistics, 1986* (Washington, D.C.: Central Intelligence Agency, 1986), tables 2 and 3, pp. 24–5 (East German per capita income $10,440, West German $10,220).

39. Dale W. Jorgenson to Daniel P. Moynihan, Mar. 18, 1991. The 1985 edition of Samuelson's *Economics* contains a table with the heading "The USSR has Grown Rapidly under Planning." The table cites the average annual growth rate of the Soviet Union's G.N.P. at 4.9% (between 1928–83), while assessing the U.S.'s growth rate at only 3.0% (between 1929–84). The text concludes that "The planned Soviet economy since 1928 has grown more rapidly than the economy of Czarist Russia and has outpaced the long-term growth of the major market economies." Paul A. Samuelson and William D. Nordhaus, *Economics* (New York: McGraw-Hill, 1985), 776. This six years before Boris Yeltsin, newly elected President of Russia, standing by a white, blue, and red Russian flag, gave a New Year's address in which he declared: "We have received a ruined country, but we must not fall into

despair. . . . Russia is seriously sick. Its economy is sick. . . .
However difficult it is for us today, we have the possibility of
crawling out of the pit in which we find ourselves." *Washington
Post*, Dec. 30, 1991, A1.

40. Gaddis, *The United States and the End of the Cold War*, 101.
41. David A. Stockman, *The Triumph of Politics: Why the Reagan
    Revolution Failed* (New York: Harper & Row, 1986), 373.
42. Lou Cannon, "An Elitist's Troubling Memoir," *Washington Post*,
    Apr. 28, 1986, A2.
43. Daniel P. Moynihan, "An Election about the Future," remarks
    before the Commonwealth Club of California, July 13, 1984, 3.
44. Daniel P. Moynihan, "The Iron Law of Emulation," in *Counting
    Our Blessings: Reflections on the Future of America* (Boston:
    Little, Brown, 1980), 115–37. The term, as the idea, is that of
    James Q. Wilson.
45. Allowance should perhaps be made for World War II, fought
    against Japan on the one hand, and the Axis powers Germany and
    Italy on the other. None of these was seen to be ethnically
    diverse, the Holocaust being overlooked or unknown. The
    enemy was seen to be motivated by ideology, Fascism (or
    Nazism), in some general way. This attitude easily carried over to
    the struggle against communism. Generals fight the last. . . .
46. George F. Kennan, "Comments on 'Kennan versus Wilson,' " in
    John Milton Cooper and Charles Neu (eds.), *The Wilson Era:
    Essays in Honor of Arthur S. Link* (Arlington Heights, Ill.: Harlan
    Davidson, 1991), 327.
47. Conversation with the author.
48. Daniel P. Moynihan, *On the Law of Nations*, 29. The quoted
    passages are from William Pfaff, *Barbarian Sentiments: How the
    American Century Ends* (New York: Hill & Wang, 1989),
    106–7.
49. Transcript of remarks by Mikhail Gorbachev before the General
    Assembly of the United Nations, Dec. 7, 1988, *Vital Speeches of
    the Day*, vol. 55, no. 8 (Feb. 1, 1989), 233.
50. Francis Fukuyama, "The End of History," *The National Interest*,
    no. 16 (Summer 1989), 3.
51. Quoted in Nathan Glazer and Daniel P. Moynihan, "Introduc-
    tion," in Glazer and Moynihan (eds.), *Ethnicity: Theory and
    Experience*, 16.

52. Ibid. 16–17.

53. Ibid. 10.

54. This was a time of some turbulence in my own affairs and I do not have anything in writing immediately at hand. However, Godfrey Hodgson, then Washington correspondent of the *Guardian*, recalls my expressing this view at that time with great conviction.

55. See Werner Sombart, *Why is There No Socialism in the United States?* (London: Macmillan, 1976) (first pub. in German in 1906).

56. James Madison, Federalist no. 10 in *The Federalist Papers* (New York: New American Library, 1961), 81.

57. Id., Federalist no. 51, in ibid. 322.

58. John Dollard, *Caste and Class in a Southern Town* (New York: Harper & Brothers, 1949), p. xiii (preface to the 1949 edn.).

59. Quoted in Bell, "Nationalism or Class?," 8 (emphasis in the original).

60. Ibid.

61. Ibid. 10.

62. Quoted in Daniel Bell, "Ethnicity and Social Change," in Glazer and Moynihan (eds.), *Ethnicity: Theory and Experience*, 174 n.

63. Bell, "Ethnicity and Social Change," in ibid. 174.

64. Donald Horowitz to Daniel P. Moynihan, Mar. 4, 1992. See also Horowitz, *Ethnic Groups in Conflict*.

65. Horowitz, *Ethnic Groups in Conflict*, 23.

CHAPTER 2: ON THE "SELF-DETERMINATION OF PEOPLES"

1. Harold Isaacs, *Idols of the Tribe: Group Identity and Political Change* (New York: Harper & Row, 1975), 32–3 (emphasis in original). In 1975, Isaacs's conference paper was published both in the book length version just cited and ·as an essay entitled "Basic Group Identity: The Idols of the Tribe," in Nathan Glazer and Daniel P. Moynihan (eds.), *Ethnicity: Theory and Experience* (Cambridge, Mass.: Harvard University Press, 1975).

2. Isaacs, *Idols of the Tribe*, 42 (emphasis in original).

3. Id., "Basic Group Identity: The Idols of the Tribe," in *Ethnicity: Theory and Experience*, 35.

4. Milton M. Gordon, *The Scope of Sociology* (Oxford: Oxford University Press, 1988), 233.

5. Isaacs, *Idols of the Tribe*, 1. Isaacs' metaphor for the ethnic "womb" is the "House of Muumbi," taken from the oath of the Kikuyu of Kenya: "I shall never leave the House of Muumbi" (the "progenital mother of the Kikuyu tribe"). "Not only in Kenya but everywhere in our world there are many Muumbis, mistresses of many such houses." Ibid.

6. Id., "Basic Group Identity," 30.

7. Id., *Idols of the Tribe*, 11.

8. Ibid. 8.

9. Ibid. 17, 19.

10. The Gulf War, as it came to be known, may well come to be seen as a prototype of the complexities of universal principles, that is to say international law, applied in a setting of intense, parochial ethnic turbulence. Horowitz records that the 1958 coup in which General Abdel Karim Qassim overthrew the Hashemite monarchy, established under the League of Nations mandate system, was a typical post-colonial act of internal aggression.

   Of the fourteen officers in Qassim's conspiracy, only two were Shiites, although Shiites comprise more than half the Iraqi population; there were no Kurdish officers in the coup group, though the Kurds comprise 15–20 percent of the Iraqi population and were not then in revolt. What little Shiite and Kurdish support Qassim had he gradually lost, and his government became essentially a Sunni regime. Successor regimes were even more narrowly identified with segments of the Sunni population.

   Horowitz adds: "Indeed, in Iraq, not merely did the Sunni minority eventually take power, but the regime became essentially the property of Saddam Hussein's family and a small clique drawn from his home village of Takrit." Donald Horowitz, *Ethnic Groups in Conflict* (Berkeley, Calif.: University of California Press, 1985), 496–7.

11. S/Res/688 (1991), Apr. 5, 1991.

12. Mario Bettati, "The Right to Interfere," *Washington Post*, Apr. 14, 1991, B7.

13. Alan Bullock, Oliver Stallybrass, and Stephen Trombley (eds.), *The Harper Dictionary of Modern Thought* (New York: Harper & Row, 1988) (2nd edn.), 766–7.

14. Samuel Johnson, "Taxation No Tyranny" (1775), quoted in Donald Greene, " 'Sweet Land of Liberty': Libertarian Rhetoric and Practice in Eighteenth-Century Britain," in Paul J. Korshin (ed.) *American Revolution & 18th Century Culture* (New York: AMS Press, 1986), 130.
15. John Augustine Wilstach, *The Works of Virgil* (Boston: Houghton, Mifflin, 1884), vol. 1, 124. The poem is *Moretum*, which literally means garden herbs.
16. Serge Schmemann, "A Blood Feud Only Worsens," *New York Times*, Mar. 8, 1992, E3.
17. *Washington Post*, Apr. 1, 1992, A25.
18. *New Yorker*, Aug. 12, 1991, p. 21.
19. Barbara F. Grimes (ed.), *Ethnologue: Languages of the World* (Dallas: Summer Institute of Linguistics, 1988) (11th edn.), p. vii.
20. Walker Connor (ed.), *Mexican Americans in Contemporary Perspective* (Washington, D.C.: Urban Institute, 1985), 2.
21. Horowitz, *Ethnic Groups in Conflict*, 166.
22. Ralf Dahrendorf, "On the Origin of Inequality Among Men," in *Essays in the Theory of Society* (Stanford, Calif.: Stanford University Press, 1968), 151–78.
23. Puerto Rico has competed in the Olympics since 1948, winning two bronze medals, both in boxing. Athletes are eligible for the team if they were born in Puerto Rico, or if they were born in the United States and have been legal residents of Puerto Rico for at least one year.
24. *San Juan Star*, Aug. 13, 1991, 14.
25. *The Encyclopaedia Britannica* (Cambridge: Cambridge University Press, 1911), vol. xxiii, p. 653.
26. Quoted in the *New York Times*, Dec. 28, 1917, 2.
27. Ibid.
28. Arthur S. Link (ed.), *The Papers of Woodrow Wilson* (Princeton, N.J.: Princeton University Press, 1984), vol. 46, p. 321.
29. Quoted in R. W. Burchfield (ed.), *A Supplement to the Oxford English Dictionary* (Oxford: Clarendon Press, 1986), vol. iv, p. 37.
30. Arthur S. Link, "Woodrow Wilson," in *World Book Encyclopedia* (Chicago: World Book Encyclopedia, 1988), vol. 21, p. 328.

31. Adolf Hitler, Berlin, Sept. 26, 1938, reprinted in Gordon W. Prange (ed.), *Hitler's Words* (Washington, D.C.: American Council on Public Affairs, 1944), 240.
32. Karl E. Meyer, "Woodrow Wilson's Dynamite: The Unabated Power of Self-Determination," *New York Times*, Aug. 14, 1991, A18.
33. Robert Lansing, Dec. 20, 1918, Lansing Papers, Manuscripts Division, Library of Congress.
34. Quoted in Charles Seymour (ed.), *The Intimate Papers of Colonel House* (Boston: Houghton Mifflin, 1928), vol. 4, p. 190.
35. Ibid. 313.
36. Robert Lansing, Dec. 30, 1918, Lansing Papers, Manuscripts Divison, Library of Congress.
37. S. Res. 48, 66th Cong., 1st Sess.
38. Text of a meeting between President Wilson and Frank P. Walsh and Edward F. Dunne, Paris, Wednesday, June 11, 1919, submitted for the record by Frank P. Walsh in testimony before the Senate Committee on Foreign Relations, *Treaty of Peace With Germany*, 66th Cong., 1st Sess. (Washington, D.C.: Government Printing Office, 1919), 838.
39. *New York Times*, Dec. 28, 1917, 2.
40. Sir Norman had, of course, written the hugely popular *The Great Illusion* (New York: G. P. Putnam's Sons, 1910), which some thought to imply that world war would not happen because it made no financial sense.
41. Thorstein Veblen, *An Inquiry into The Nature of Peace and the Terms of its Perpetuation* (New York: Augustus M. Kelley, 1964), 41 (first pub. in 1917).
42. Joseph Dorfman, "Two Unpublished Papers of Thorstein Veblen on the Nature of Peace" in *Political Science Quarterly*, vol. 47 (June 1932), 185.
43. Thorstein Veblen, "An Outline of a Policy for the Control of the 'Economic Penetration' of Backward Countries and of Foreign Investments," *Political Science Quarterly*, vol. 47 (June 1932) (written in 1917).
44. Ibid. 194.
45. It was Churchill, of course, who declared in a Nov. 1942 speech at the Lord Mayor's Day Luncheon in London: "I have

not become the King's First Minister in order to preside over the liquidation of the British Empire."

46. The term Aryan, from the Sanskrit for upper caste, was popularized by the German-born philologist Max Müller to describe the European family of languages that he and others had supposedly traced to the Indus Valley.

47. To take but one, telling example, according to Harold Butler's unpublished memoirs, Roosevelt enthusiastically cleared out offices in the Navy Department for use by Butler during the founding conference of the International Labor Organization in Washington. Roosevelt historian Frank Friedel has written: "[The] whole episode had eluded me when I wrote my volume about FDR in the Navy Department. Nor is it in Geoffrey Ward's compendious volume covering the period [*A First-Class Temperament: The Emergence of Franklin Roosevelt* (New York: Harper & Row, 1989)]." Frank Friedel to Daniel P. Moynihan, Dec. 4, 1990. A full discussion of this episode is contained in Daniel P. Moynihan, *On the Law of Nations* (Cambridge, Mass.: Harvard University Press, 1990), 61–3.

48. Roosevelt's activities in connection with the League are discussed in greater detail in *On the Law of Nations,* 56–68.

49. Ruth Russell, *A History of the United Nations Charter* (Washington, D.C.: Brookings Institution, 1958), 75–6.

50. Interestingly, "improved labor standards" did make it into the text. Roosevelt first became involved with the I.L.O. in Washington in 1918, and had taken the United States into that organization, the only League body it did join, in 1934.

51. This ambiguity in the Atlantic Charter allowed the two signatories their own different interpretations: "The Americans held that the article's concept of self-determination had universal application, including the right of colonies to become independent. . . . The British took a narrower view. Speaking in Parliament on 9 September 1941, Churchill stated that—as far as Britain was concerned—the article applied only to territories seized by the Nazis, and not to the [British] Empire." Dennis Kux, *India and the United States: The Estranged Democracies, 1941–91* (MS, Dec. 1991), 11–12 (forthcoming, Washington: National Defense University Press).

52. Evelyn Waugh, *A Tourist in Africa* (Boston: Little, Brown, 1960), 157.

53. Russell, *A History of the United Nations Charter*, 811.
54. Ibid. 813 n.
55. Quoted ibid. 812–13.
56. Quoted ibid. 823–4.
57. Ibid. 831.
58. George Will, "Gorbachev's Barren Strategy," *Washington Post*, Aug. 23, 1991, A19.
59. See Richard D. Alba's superb statistical analysis *Ethnic Identity: The Transformation of White America 1990* (New Haven, Conn.: Yale University Press, 1990). Alba notes that three out of every four marriages among whites in the United States involve some degree of ethnic boundary crossing, and that about half of all marriages among whites in the United States occur between individuals whose ancestries differ completely. Ibid. 12.
60. Benjamin Franklin, *Writings* (New York: Literary Classics of the United States, 1987), 374. The leading Franklin scholars inform me that there is no indication that Franklin is being ironic here.
61. Dale T. Knobel, *Paddy and the Republic: Ethnicity and Nationality in Antebellum America* (Middletown, Conn.: Wesleyan University Press, 1986).
62. See generally, ibid., which, as Knobel describes it, "is not a book about the Irish in antebellum America; it is a book about the popular image of the Irish in antebellum America, which was quite another thing. It suggests that serial images of the Irish were closely related to evolving notions about ethnicity and, especially, the nature of American nationality." Ibid. 3.
63. Woodrow Wilson, Sept. 18, 1919, quoted in Arthur S. Link (ed.), *The Papers of Woodrow Wilson* (Princeton, N.J.: Princeton University Press, 1990), vol. 63, 348.
64. Walter Lippmann, *The Stakes of Diplomacy* (New York: Holt, 1915), 9–10.
65. Diary of Colonel Edward M. House, vol. 13 (Jan. 1, 1918–July 8, 1918), Feb. 28, 1918, 80, in the Edward M. House Papers, Manuscripts and Archives Division, Yale University Library.
66. The almanac used by House was consistent with other contemporaneous estimates. See *The American Jewish Year Book* (Philadelphia: Jewish Publication Society of America, 1919), 600 (15, 121, 319 Jews in the world).

67. Charles Seymour, *Letters From the Paris Peace Conference* (New Haven, Conn.: Yale University Press, 1965), 250.

68. Nigel Nicolson (ed.), *Vita and Harold: The Letters of Vita Sackville-West and Harold Nicolson* (New York: Putnam, 1992), 83.

69. Paul Kennedy, *The Rise and Fall of the Great Powers* (New York: Random House, 1987), 216.

70. Russell, *A History of the United Nations Charter*, 102. The passage Russell quotes is from the letter to Field Marshal Smuts, which is dated Nov. 24, 1942.

71. Reston's articles on the conference appeared in the *New York Times* between Aug. 23 and Oct. 2, 1944. Reston was immeasurably aided by the generosity of a member of the Chinese (Nationalist) delegation, who gave him the full texts of proposals being considered by the U.S., British, Soviet, and Chinese delegations. See James Reston, *Deadline: A Memoir* (New York: Random House, 1991), 134.

72. Russell, *A History of the United Nations Charter*, 434.

73. Ibid. 538.

74. Quoted ibid. 596–7 n. (emphasis in the original).

75. Samuel Rosenman (ed.), *The Public Papers and Addresses of Franklin D. Roosevelt* (New York: Harper & Brothers, 1950), vol. 1944–5 ("Victory and the Threshold of Peace"), 611.

CHAPTER 3: NATIONAL PROLETARIAN INTERNATIONALISM

1. Vernon V. Aspaturian, *The Union Republics in Soviet Diplomacy: A Study of Soviet Federalism in the Service of Soviet Foreign Policy* (Paris: L'Institut Universitaire des Hautes Études Internationales, 1960), 15.

2. Ibid. 16.

3. Ibid. 18.

4. R. W. Burchfield (ed.), *A Supplement to the Oxford English Dictionary* (Oxford: Clarendon Press, 1986), vol. iv, p. 37.

5. Quoted in Edward Hallett Carr, *The Bolshevik Revolution: 1917–1923* (New York: Macmillan, 1951), vol. 1, p. 416.

6. The actual text, however, reads slightly differently. The exact phrase "self-determination" does not appear. Instead, the proclamation asserts "the right of every people to dispose of

itself." *The General Council of the First International, 1864–1866: The London Conference, 1865, Minutes* (Moscow: Foreign Languages Publishing House, 1963), 246. This at first appears to be an awkward translation of the more precise "self-determination." However, in correspondence with the Moscow archivists of the originals of these early communist documents, I have verified that "the right of every nation to dispose of itself" is the original phrase used in English at the 1865 London conference. (Correspondence in my possession.) Obviously the substance of both phrases is the same.

7. Quoted in Carr, *The Bolshevik Revolution*, 416.

8. Walker Connor, *The National Question in Marxist-Leninist Theory and Strategy* (Princeton, N.J.: Princeton University Press, 1984), 11.

9. Ibid.

10. Robert Conquest, *Stalin: Breaker of Nations* (New York: Viking Penguin, 1991), 52–3.

11. The Congress called itself the "International Socialist Workers and Trade Union Congress," *Verhandlungen und Beschlüsse des internationalen sozialistichen Arbeiter und Gewerkschafts-Kongresses zu London, vom 27. Juli bis 1. August 1896* (Berlin: Expedition der Buchhandlung Vorwarts, 1896).

In his essay, "The Right of Nations to Self-Determination," which first appeared in the spring of 1914, Lenin cites a resolution passed by the Second International in 1896. (This English trans. is from the *Collected Works*, published in Moscow in 1964. The German terms were in the original.)

This Congress declares that it stands for the full right of all nations to self-determination [*Selbstbestimmungsrecht*] and expresses its sympathy for the workers of every country now suffering under the yoke of military, national or other absolutism. This Congress calls upon the workers of all these countries to join the ranks of class-conscious [*Klassenbewußte*] workers of the whole world in order jointly to fight for the defeat of international capitalism and for the achievement of the aims of international Social-Democracy.

Quoted in V. I. Lenin, "The Right of Nations to Self-Determination," in *V. I. Lenin: Collected Works*, vol. 20 (Moscow: Progress Publishers, 1964), 430–1.

12. Quoted in Conquest, *Stalin: Breaker of Nations*, 53.
13. V. I. Lenin, "The Nationalist Question in Our Programme," *V. I. Lenin: Selected Works* (Moscow: Co-operative Publishing Society of Foreign Workers in the U.S.S.R., 1934), vol. ii, p. 322 (first pub. in *Iskra*, July 15, 1903).
14. Bohdan Nahaylo and Victor Swoboda, *Soviet Disunion: A History of the Nationalities Problem in the USSR* (New York: Macmillan, 1990), 14.
15. George F. Kennan, *Around the Cragged Hill* (New York: W. W. Norton, 1992), 73 (uncorrected proofs).
16. Lenin, "The National Question in Our Programme," 322.
17. Aspaturian, *The Union Republics in Soviet Diplomacy*, 55.
18. Quoted in Nahaylo and Swoboda, *Soviet Disunion*, 14.
19. V. I. Lenin, "Theses on the National Question," in *V. I. Lenin: Collected Works* (Moscow: Foreign Languages Publishing House, 1963), vol. 19, pp. 243–4 (written in 1913) (emphasis in original).
20. Ibid. 244.
21. Jonathan Yardley, "Warmth From the North," *Washington Post*, Oct. 2, 1991, B2.
22. Aspaturian, *The Union Republics in Soviet Diplomacy*, 54.
23. E. J. Hobsbawm, *Nations and Nationalism since 1780: Programme, Myth, Reality* (Cambridge: Cambridge University Press, 1990), 2.
24. Ibid.
25. Ibid. 2 n.
26. Richard Pipes, *The Formation of the Soviet Union: Communism and Nationalism, 1917–1923* (Cambridge, Mass.: Harvard University Press, 1954), 36–7.
27. Isaac Deutscher, *Stalin: A Political Biography* (New York: Oxford University Press, 1949), 177. The question of nationality is complex, but if one goes strictly by place of birth, it appears that the Council consisted of nine pure Russians, one border-area Russian, four Ukrainians, and one Georgian. Again, on the basis of birthplace, that means that there were fourteen Slavs and one Georgian on the Council:

    V. I. Lenin: Russian. Born 1870 in Simbirsk, Russia. Chairman.

    A. I. Rykov: Russian. Born 1881 in Saratov, Russia. Commissar of Internal Affairs.

L. D. Trotsky: Ukrainian. Born 1879 in vil Yanovka, Kherson Province, Ukraine. Commissar of Foreign Affairs. (Son of Jewish colonist.)

V. Lunacharskiy: Ukrainian. Born 1875 in Poltava, Ukraine. Commissar of Education.

G. Lomov: Russian. Born 1888 in Saratov, Russia. Commissar of Justice. (Born G. I. Oppokov.)

Josif Stalin: Georgian. Born 1879 in Gori, Georgia. Commissar of Nationalities. (Born Joseph Djugashvili.)

V. P. Nogin: Russian. Born 1878 in Moscow, Russia. Commissar of Trade and Industry.

V. A. Anatov-Ovseyenko: Ukrainian. Born 1884 in Chernigov, Ukraine. Military Commissar.

N. V. Krylenko: Russian. Born 1885 in vil Bekhteyevka, Russia. Military Commissar.

P. E. Dybenko: Ukrainian. Born 1889 in vil Lyudkov, Chernigov Province, Ukraine. Military Commissar.

I. A. Teodorovich: Russian. Born 1875 in Smolensk, Russia. Commissar of Foodstuffs.

V. P. Miliutin: Russian-Ukrainian. Born 1884 in Aleksandrovo, Kursk Province, border of Russia and Ukraine. Commissar of Arable Farming.

N. P. Avilov: Russian. Born 1887 in Kaluga, Russia. Commissar of Posts and Telegraphs.

A. G. Shliapnikov: Russian. Born 1884 in Murom, Vladimir Province, Russia. Commissar of Labor.

I. I. Skvortsov: Russian. Born 1870 in Bogorodsk, Russia. Commissar of Finance. (Pen name: Stepanov.)

It appears that Lenin's maternal grandfather Alexander Blank was Jewish. In 1992 the *Moscow News* published correspondence with Stalin in which Lenin's sister Anna Ulyanovna-Yelizarova urged that this fact be made public in order to combat growing anti-Semitism "even among Communists." Stalin demurred. Lenin's sister retorted that this "does not follow logically from recognition of the complete equality of nations." Further, that Lenin had a high estimation of "Jewish revolutionary spirit compared to the weak and passive Russian character." Quoted in *Jerusalem Post*, March 2, 1992, 12.

28. Quoted in Deutscher, *Stalin*, 182.

29. Ibid. 182–3.

30. Nathan Glazer, *The Social Basis of American Communism* (New York: Harcourt, Brace & World, 1961), 22–3. Likewise socialist Zionists carried the faith to Israel where the Israeli Labor Party has only just given up the red flag and the "Internationale." Michael Walzer, "The Turn," *New Republic*, Sept. 26, 1992, 14.

31. Joseph Stalin, *Marxism and the National and Colonial Question* (Moscow: Co-operative Publishing Society of Foreign Workers in the U.S.S.R., 1935), 48.

32. Ibid. 8.

33. Ibid. 33.

34. Quoted in Deutscher, *Stalin*, 185.

35. Stalin, *Marxism and the National and Colonial Question* 15.

36. George F. Will, "1982: Oh, Well," *Newsweek*, Jan. 3, 1983, 68.

37. Aleksandr Solzhenitsyn, *Rebuilding Russia: Reflections and Tentative Proposals* (New York: Farrar, Straus, and Giroux, 1991), 6–7.

38. Ibid. 21.

39. Ibid. 14.

40. Ibid. 10 (emphasis in the original).

41. Transcript of an address by Pyotr K. Kravchanka before the Forty-Sixth Session of the United Nations General Assembly, New York, Sept. 26, 1991, 8.

42. Transcript of an address by Askar Akayev, President of the Republic of Kyrgyzstan, before the Committee on Foreign Relations in the United States Senate, Oct. 23, 1991, 3.

43. *Washington Post*, Nov. 8, 1991, A30.

44. Hobsbawm, *Nations and Nationalism*, 172–3.

45. Walker Connor to Daniel P. Moynihan, Nov. 4, 1991.

CHAPTER 4: BEFORE THE FALL

1. See David Fromkin, *A Peace to End All Peace: The Fall of the Ottoman Empire and the Creation of the Modern Middle East* (New York: Avon Books, 1989), 343. Reprinted by permission of Henry Holt and Co.

2. A secret pact providing for the dismantling of the Ottoman Empire, the Sykes-Picot agreement, among other things, placed a portion of Palestine under joint Allied command and allowed for

the recognition of an independent Arab state whose territory would be split into French and British areas of influence.

3. Fromkin, *A Peace to End All Peace*, 343.

4. Ibid. 345.

5. Ibid. 344. Amery was on the staff of the War Cabinet, which Lloyd George headed.

6. Ibid. 450–1.

7. Martin Peretz, *New Republic*, Aug. 3, 1992, 8.

8. George F. Kennan, *Around the Cragged Hill* (New York: W. W. Norton, 1992), 71 (uncorrected proofs).

9. Elie Kedourie, " 'Minorities,' " in *The Chatham House Version and Other Middle-Eastern Studies* (New York: Praeger Publishers, 1970), 302.

10. Quoted ibid. 302–3.

11. Ibid. 305.

12. Ibid. 303.

13. Ibid. 301.

14. M. Eliade (ed.), *The Encyclopedia of Religion* (New York: Macmillan, 1987), vol. 10, p. 370.

15. Aleksandr Solzhenitsyn, *Rebuilding Russia: Reflections and Tentative Proposals* (New York: Farrar, Straus, and Giroux, 1991), 14.

16. Nicholas D. Kristof, "Restlessness Reaches Mongols in China," *New York Times*, July 19, 1992, E3.

17. Solomon Bloom, "The Peoples of My Hometown: Before Nationalism Crushed Rumania's Design for Living," *Commentary*, Apr. 1947 329.

18. Ibid. 330.

19. Ibid. 330–1.

20. Ibid. 331.

21. Ibid.

22. Solzhenitsyn, *Rebuilding Russia*, 6.

23. Daniel P. Moynihan, "What Wretched Refuse?," *New York Magazine*, May 12, 1986, 59.

24. Bloom, "The Peoples of My Hometown," 334–5.

25. Evelyn Waugh, *A Tourist in Africa* (Boston: Little, Brown, 1960), 157.

26. Quoted in "Two Concepts of Nationalism: An Interview with Isaiah Berlin," *New York Review of Books*, Nov. 21, 1991, 22.

27. Ibid. 19.
28. Ibid. 23.

CHAPTER 5: ORDER IN AN AGE OF CHAOS

1. Transcript of remarks by Boris N. Yeltsin, President of the Russian Federation, before a Joint Session of the Congress of the United States, June 17, 1992.
2. *The Economist*, Dec. 21, 1991, 11.
3. Ibid.
4. C. P. Cavafy, "Expecting the Barbarian," *The Complete Poems of Cavafy* (New York: Harcourt, Brace & World, 1961), (trans. by R. Dalven, introduction by W. H. Auden), 18–19.
5. *New York Times*, July 22, 1992, A18.
6. *Washington Post*, Aug. 4, 1992, A11.
7. *The Economist*, Aug. 8, 1992, 37.
8. Francis Fukuyama, "The Beginning of Foreign Policy," *The New Republic*, Aug. 17 and 24, 1992, 24.
9. Quoted ibid. 25.
10. W. R. Connor, "Why Were We Surprised?", *American Scholar*, Spring 1991, 176. W. R. Connor is the Director of the National Humanities Center at Research Triangle Park, North Carolina. Walker Connor, whom I have cited frequently in this and other works, is the John R. Reitemeyer Professor of Political Science at Trinity College, Connecticut.
11. Romans 2:9 (Revised Standard Version).
12. Reinhold Niebuhr, "Law, Conscience, and Grace," in *Justice and Mercy* (San Francisco: Harper & Row, 1974), 41. The sermon concerned individual behavior in collective settings, the central theme of Niebuhr's finest work, *Moral Man and Immoral Society*. Now a New Yorker, he followed ethnic matters with great care and concern. I have never known such courage and kindness as he showed me at a time of fierce intolerance in the summer of 1965.
13. W. H. Auden, "Introduction," in *The Complete Poems of Cavafy*, p. xiii.
14. Fukuyama, "The Beginning of Foreign Policy," 25.
15. James Crawford, *The Creation of States in International Law* (Oxford: Clarendon Press, 1979), 3.
16. Ibid. 31.

17. Hans Kelsen, "Recognition in International Law—Theoretical Observations," *American Journal of International Law*, vol. 35, no. 4 (Oct. 1941), 605. Among the numerous works on this subject, the leading "constitutive" text is probably H. Lauterpacht, *Recognition in International Law* (Cambridge: Cambridge University Press, 1947) and the leading "declaratory" work is T. C. Chen, *The International Law of Recognition* (London: Stevens, 1951).

18. Michael Akehurst, *A Modern Introduction to International Law* (London: Allen & Unwin, 1987), 57.

19. Crawford, *The Creation of States*, 85.

20. The Aaland Islands Question, *Report Presented to the Council of the League by the Commission of Rapporteurs*, League of Nations Doc. B.7.21/68/106 (Apr. 16, 1921), 27–8.

21. Crawford, *The Creation of States*, 85–7.

22. *Yearbook of the United Nations—1960* (New York: Columbia University Press, 1961), 48.

23. Reprinted in L. Sohn and T. Buergenthal (eds.), *Basic Documents on International Protection of Human Rights* (New York: Bobbs-Merrill, 1973), 116–17.

24. The former "rule" against supporting insurgencies was reinforced by the International Court of Justice in *Nicaragua* v. *United States*, *I.C.J. Reports* 1986, 14.

25. British India was an original member, joining Oct. 30, 1945. Pakistan was admitted on Sept. 30, 1947. Bangladesh became a member on Sept. 17, 1974.

26. Reprinted in L. Sohn and T. Buergenthal (eds.), *Basic Documents on International Protection of Human Rights*, 30–4.

27. Akehurst, *A Modern Introduction to International Law*, 295. This perhaps oversimplifies concerning the Moroccan position. For example, before the International Court of Justice Morocco relied upon the inconsistency in Resolution 1514 I have already discussed. Morocco conceded that paragraph 2 of Resolution 1514 created a right of self-determination, but argued that this was only one of "two basic principles" in the resolution, which needed to be balanced against "the principles of the national unity and territorial integrity of countries, enunciated in paragraph 6 of the same resolution." *I.C.J. Reports* 1975, 12.

By comparison, during the Security Council debate on Dec. 15, 1975 concerning the situation in East Timor, the Indonesian representative, Anwar Sani, stated:

> Indonesia's reaction to the wish for complete integration [with Indonesia] as represented by APODETI [an East Timorese political party] was that it would welcome such a decision if it were to be the outcome of a free and democratic exercise of the right of self-determination by the entire people of Portuguese Timor in accordance with General Assembly resolutions 1514 (XV) and 1541 (XV). Indonesia emphasized that it had no claim on Portuguese Timor, but that if the people of the Territory decided freely and democratically to become independent through integration with the unitary State of Indonesia, Indonesia would welcome it. . . .
>
> We who have taken the right of self-determination into our own hands and have defended it with our lives and blood have certainly no intention of denying it to others.

S.C.O.R., 30th year, 1,864th meeting (Dec. 15, 1975), paras. 71, 75. See Daniel P. Moynihan, *A Dangerous Place* (Boston: Little, Brown, 1978), 245–7, and id., "Abiotrophy in Turtle Bay: The United Nations in 1975," *Harvard International Law Journal*, vol. 17, no. 3 (Summer 1976), 469–70.

28. An overlooked precedent of large import is that of Rhodesia. In 1962 the General Assembly determined that Rhodesia was "Non-Self-Governing," and the Security Council, acting under Article 41, *ordered* states not to recognize or establish diplomatic relations. In time, white Rhodesia was no more.

29. Moynihan, *A Dangerous Place*, 244–5.

30. Graham E. Fuller, *The Democracy Trap: Perils of the Post-Cold War World* (New York: Penguin, 1991), 98.

31. "Agreement on Ending the War and Restoring Peace in Vietnam," Jan. 27, 1973, U.S.-Viet., art. 9, 935 U.N.T.S. 52, 55.

32. Ibid.

33. Walker Connor, "Ethnology and the Peace of South Asia," *World Politics*, vol. xxii, no. 1 (Oct. 1969), 51–86.

34. Quoted ibid. 62.

35. Quoted ibid. 63.

36. Ibid. 68.
37. Donald L. Horowitz, *Ethnic Groups in Conflict* (Berkeley, Calif.: University of California Press, 1985), 13.
38. Ainslee T. Embree, "Indian Civilization and Regional Cultures: The Two Realities," in Paul Wallace (ed.), *Region and Nation in India* (New Delhi: Oxford University Press, 1985), 30.
39. See Daniel P. Moynihan, "The United States in Opposition," *Commentary*, vol. 59, Mar. 1975, 31–44.
40. Quoted in Dennis Kux, *India and the United States: The Estranged Democracies, 1941–91* (MS, Dec. 1991), 11–12 (forthcoming, Washington: National Defense University Press).
41. Embree, "Indian Civilization and Regional Cultures," 23–4.
42. T. K. Tope, *The Constitution of India* (Bombay: Popular Prakashan, 1971), 450.
43. Article 340 reads:

    (1) The President may by order appoint a Commission consisting of such persons as he thinks fit to investigate the conditions of socially and educationally backward classes within the territory of India and the difficulties under which they labor and to make recommendations as to the steps that should be taken by the Union or any State to remove such difficulties and to improve their condition and as to the grants that should be made for the purpose by the Union or any State and the conditions subject to which such grants should be made, and the order appointing such Commission shall define the procedure to be followed by the Commission.

44. *The Mandal Commission Report: Selected Chapters from the Report of the Backward Classes Commission, 1980* (Bombay: Centre for Monitoring Indian Economy, Sept. 1990), 1. The finest intentions—which cannot be doubted of the Nehru generation—are easily enough elided. Tope records:

    When the Backward Class Commission was appointed many communities which are rich and well placed in life expressed their desire [to be] included in the list of the Backward Class Communities. An interesting classification of Backward Classes came from the State of Mysore where 95% of the total population was classified as backward and the classification was based on considerations of religion and castes rather than on economic backwardness or cultural backwardness. The list of

backward classes drawn by Mysore Government contained all communities and castes of Hindus except Brahmins, Banias and Kayasthas and all other communities except Anglo-Indians and Parsis. (Tope, 453).
Banias are a Hindu caste of merchants and traders, Kayasthas of clerks and accountants. Parsis, alternatively Parsees, are descended from Mithraic Persians. The author mercifully reports that the Mysore High Court struck down this all-inclusive classification, but the disposition was present at the creation.

45. *The Mandal Commission Report*, 18 (quoting J. R. Kamble, *Rise and Awakening of Depressed Classes in India* (New Delhi: National Publishing House, 1971)).

46. Quoted ibid. 3.

47. Jyotirindra Das Gupta, "Ethnicity, Democracy and Development in India," in Atul Kohli (ed.), *India's Democracy: An Analysis of Changing State–Society Relations* (Princeton, N.J.: Princeton University Press, 1988), 146.

48. Sanjay Yadav, "The Mandal Milestone: Class and Caste in the 1990's," paper presented at Oxford University, Nov. 21, 1991, 16.

49. Ibid. 2.

50. *Times of India*, Jan. 4, 1992, 8.

51. Embree, "Indian Civilization and Regional Cultures," 35.

52. Ibid. 36. The chakra is a multi-spoke wheel emblazoned on the center of the Indian tricolor flag. It represents the Wheel of Enlightenment of Buddhism and is associated with Asoka, the third century B.C. Mauryan king who embraced Buddhism. It can also be a spinning wheel, a symbol of Gandhian simplicity and self-reliance.

53. Harold Isaacs to Wallace Irwin Jr., Dec. 23, 1981. (Correspondence in my possession.)

54. Ibid.

55. Id. eid., May 30, 1983.

56. Id. eid., Jan. 12, 1984.

57. Fukuyama, "The Beginning of Foreign Policy," 24.

58. Ibid. 25.

59. Secretary of State James A. Baker III, " 'First Amendment' Freedoms in Central and Eastern Europe," *Dispatch*, vol. 2, no. 26 (July 1, 1991), 463.

60. Transcript of remarks by President George Bush before the Supreme Soviet of the Ukrainian Soviet Socialist Republic, Aug. 1, 1991, 3.
61. Stansfield Turner, "Intelligence for a New World Order," *Foreign Affairs*, vol. 70, no. 4 (Fall 1991), 162.
62. Transcript of remarks delivered by Robert M. Gates, Director of Central Intelligence, at the Foreign Policy Association, May 20, 1992, 29. In a paper presented to the 1992 meeting of the American Sociological Association, Seymour Martin Lipset stated: "The basic question which social scientists have to deal with in reacting to the collapse of Communism in the Soviet Union is why they, and, it must be admitted, other non-academic experts such as the intelligence agencies of the great Western powers, did not anticipate that this would happen, or even that it could occur." (Seymour Martin Lipset, "Anticipations of the Failure of Communism," (unpub. MS), 1.) Another sociologist, Randall Collins, writes that "The mind-set of both right and left seemed to be against recognizing any possibility of Russian vulnerability." (Randall Collins to Daniel P. Moynihan, Sept. 22, 1992.) A 1980 paper by Collins depicted the system as exceedingly vulnerable, not least on ethnic grounds. The editors of *Science* declined even to send it out for review. In 1982 an article in *Foreign Affairs* assured readers that "The Soviet Union is not now nor will it be during the next decade in the throes of a true systemic crisis, for it boasts enormous unused reserves of political and social stability. . . ." (Seweryn Bialer and Joan Afferica, "Reagan and Russia," *Foreign Affairs*, vol. 61, no. 5 (Winter 1982–3), 263.)
63. Quoted in Peter Gay, "A Master Diplomat and a Good Hater," *New York Times Book Review*, Jan. 26, 1992, 12 (review of Otto Pflanze, *Bismarck and the Development of Germany*.)
64. *The Economist*, July 18, 1992, 35–7.
65. *New York Times*, July 21, 1992, A8.
66. *Roll Call*, July 30, 1992, 1.
67. Horowitz, *Ethnic Groups in Conflict*, 675.
68. Milton M. Gordon, *Assimilation in American Life: The Role of Race, Religion, and National Origins* (New York: Oxford University Press, 1964), 133 (citing Marcus Hansen, *The Immigrant in American Society*, (Cambridge, Mass.: Harvard University Press, 1940), 132).

INDEX

Hmong territory 157
Ho Chi Minh 52, 53, 156, 158
Hobsbawm, E. J. 28, 115,
  124–5
Hofstadter, Richard 31
Hohenzollerns 90, 128, 135
Holland, John P. 14
homogeneity 140, 168
Horowitz, Donald L. 11, 119
  Ethnic Groups in Conflict 27,
  28, 61–2, 72, 157, 171–2
House, Colonel E. M. 82, 88,
  101, 102
Houston 171
Howe, Frederic C. 86
Hull, Cordell 104
human rights 6, 147, 152
humanitarian law 67, 173
Humphrey, Hubert H. 45–6
Hungary 72, 139
Husain (Prophet's
  grandson) 67, 119

Iceland 72
Ichud 33
idealism 77
identity 27, 42, 65, 169
  psychological role of 64
  social class and 28
Ikle, Fred 147
Illyrians 3
immigration 2, 118, 136–7,
  140, 172
  illegal 170
imperialism, *see* colonialism
  inevitable victory of socialism
  over 124
independence 73, 76, 78, 79,
  156, 158
  Finnish 117
  Indian 159, 162
  Irish 14
  Slovene and Croat 166

Independent, the 24
India 14, 37, 132, 157, 159–65
  British 151
Indonesia 152, 153
industrialization 110
infant mortality 40
Intercollegiate Socialist
  Society 86
International:
  First 108, 111
  Second 109, 112
International Commission of
  Jurists 149
International Court of
  Justice 71
*International Encyclopedia of the
  Social Sciences* 22
International Geographical
  Union 168
International Institute for
  Strategic Studies 16
international law 15, 67, 71, 77,
  145, 148–9
  Kuwait and 9, 66
internationalism 19, 28,
  107–26, 155
IRA (Irish Republican Army) 24
Iran 46, 67, 68
Iraq 66, 76, 128, 165
  see also Kurds
Ireland 14, 85, 99, 109, 132
  Northern xi, 24, 76
  see also Irish (people)
Irgun 33
Irian Jaya 152
Irish (people):
  American, stereotype of 99
  Catholic 14, 84, 136, 140
  charitable organizations in
  New York 172
  'Famine' 136
Isaacs, Harold R. 25, 63, 64, 65,
  165

United Nations xiv, 6, 36, 40,
71–6 *passim*, 90, 94, 131
An Agenda for Peace
(Boutros-Ghali) xv-xvi
Charter 4, 9, 15, 66, 67–8,
69, 71, 81, 93, 95, 97, 145,
149, 150, 151, 153, 168
General Assembly xvi, 37, 53,
72, 74, 80, 105, 106, 150,
151, 158
High Commissioner for
Refugees 20
Security Council 18, 66, 67,
68, 104, 152, 158
seminar on Multinational
Societies (1965) 56
troops: in Somalia 16; in
Yugoslavia 21
Universal Declaration of
Human Rights 152
United States xii–xiii, 6, 11, 17,
18, 24, 34, 37, 68, 159,
169–70
allegations of American
colonialism 76
American Communist Party
45, 118
arms control agreement with
USSR successor states 35
Bureau of the Census 40
Congress 5, 12, 73, 74–5,
78–9, 80, 143, 170, 172
Delegation to Negotiations
on Nuclear and Space Arms
45
failure to forecast the
magnitude of the Soviet
crisis 167
foreign policy xiv, 46, 147
GNP 48
immigration 2, 118, 136–7,
140, 172; illegal 170
interest in new world order 9

motto 70
Navy 14
opinion on territorial integrity
of Yugoslavia 166
Red scare 85
Senate 23, 36, 42, 44, 51,
145; Committee on Foreign
Relations 84, 122; Select
Committee on
Intelligence 38, 41
State Department 57
steel production 138
see also Chicago; Los Angeles;
New York; San Francisco;
Washington
University of Chicago 29, 33
University of Tübingen 72
USSR, *see* Soviet Union

Vandenberg, Arthur H.
(Senator) 105
Veblen, Thorstein 87, 88, 89,
90, 140
Versailles Peace Treaty
(1919) 72
Vienna 86, 102
uprising (1848) 109
Vietnam 154, 155, 156
Virgil 70

Walsh, Frank P. 84, 85
War Crimes Commission 103
Warner, W. L. 29
Washington 7, 39, 43, 55, 57,
108
Washington Post 50, 123
Watt, Donald Cameron 69
Waugh, Evelyn 93, 141
Weber, Eugen 2
Weber, Max 1, 61, 168
Western Sahara 71, 152, 153
Westphalian state 12, 97
White Russia, *see* Belarus

Index compiled by Frank Pert